GOOD GUYS & BAD GUYS

GOOD GUYS & BAD GUYS

Profiles and histories of the production of twenty-nine action-packed classics featuring the Good Guys and the Bad Guys, illustrated with production shots and stills from the actual movies as well as posters and contemporary publicity shots.

Edited by Ann Lloyd

Galahad Books · New York

Title page: Warren Beatty in Warner Brothers'
Bonnie and Clyde, 1967

© 1982 Orbis Publishing Limited, London
Published by Galahad Books
95 Madison Avenue
New York, New York 10016

ISBN: 0-88365-628-0

Printed in Italy

Many of the illustrations come from stills issued to
publicize films made or distributed by the
following companies: Columbia, Ealing, EMI,
MGM, Paramount, PEA/Les Artistes Associés,
Rank Organisation, RKO, David O. Selznick,
Stanley Kramer Productions, Toho, 20th Century-
Fox, United Artists, Universal, Warner Brothers.
Although every effort is being made to trace the
present copyright holders, we apologize in
advance for any unintentional omission or neglect
and will be pleased to insert the appropriate
acknowledgment to companies or individuals in
any subsequent edition of this publication.

Acknowledgments: Michel Ciment, Greg Edwards
Archive, Joel Finler Collection, Ronald Grant
Archive, Harris Films Ltd., David Hine, Kobal
Collection, National Film Archive, David Robinson,
Talisman Books.

CONTENTS

THE THIN MAN

FILM WEEKLY, November 9, 1934

William POWELL · Myrna LOY in *The* **THIN MAN** Cert 'A'

A Metro-Goldwyn-Mayer PICTURE

A LAUGH TOPS EVERY THRILLING MOMENT

. . . a new kind of mystery with more laughs than chills . . more warm-blooded romance than cold-blooded murder! Hilariously gay! Breathlessly exciting!

WITH

MAUREEN O'SULLIVAN

Nat Pendleton . . . Minna Gombell.

"A thriller that for sheer pace, fun and efficiency leaves all others standing. Don't miss this very bright spot."
The Observer

"Head and shoulders above anything I have seen in months . . . ought to be by miles the most popular film of the year."
Sunday Pictorial

The thin man of the title is both suspect and victim, but he makes only the briefest of appearances at the beginning of the film. Yet, like Baron Frankenstein, he lingered on in the titles of a whole series of films to become erroneously associated with their leading character, Nick Charles. Presumably the use of the thin man in the titles of the five sequels (*After the Thin Man*, 1936; *Another Thin Man*, 1939; *Shadow of the Thin Man*, 1941; *The Thin Man Goes Home*, 1944; *Song of the Thin Man*, 1947), was felt by MGM to be a guarantee of a successful box-office.

The chemistry of the original film works brilliantly. Its mixture of sophisticated comedy, romance and detective story was exactly to the taste of contemporary audiences and its appeal is durable: when *The Thin Man* was shown for the first time in West Germany in 1969 it ran for more than ten weeks in some towns.

The complications of the 'whodunnit' plot are of no real interest. Frances Goodrich and Albert Hackett, one of several husband-and-wife writing teams who have contributed so much to American show business, made an intelligent adaptation of the novel by Dashiell Hammett whose convoluted plot was essentially unsuited to the screen. Their solution to the structural problem was the elaborate dinner-party sequence which does not occur in the book, and although it is not entirely satisfactory it at least disposes of the loose ends so quickly that the audience is unlikely to spot any flaws. In any case no-one is expected to take the murder and mayhem seriously and indeed the unpleasantness of some of Hammett's characters has been considerably softened. The special flavour of the film lies in the snap and crackle of the dialogue, which neatly captures Hammett's laconic style, and in the characterization of the two principals.

Nick Charles, Hammett's delightful detective, has none of the irritating self-righteousness of Raymond Chandler's hero, Philip Marlowe. In fact he seems to have a great deal in common with his creator. Not quite a drunk, Nick is nevertheless happily but inoffensively pickled most of the time, although alcohol seems to stimulate the detecting process:

Nick and Nora, as represented by William Powell and Myrna Loy, have so much careless charm that it is very easy to overlook the flimsiness of the plot. Powell in particular puts over a fantastic confidence trick: the silky voice, the insouciant gaiety, the faultless timing, lend an air of authenticity to a set of wildly improbable incidents, and Miss Loy's matter-of-fact acceptance of each new crisis, her unruffled elegance and quick sympathy complete a relationship in which one gladly believes if only because of its pleasant air of mature sensuality. This was their second film as a team, the first being *Manhattan Melodrama* also made in 1934 by Van Dyke, to whom must go the credit for realizing their potential in spite of opposition from Louis B. Mayer. In all they played together 14 times, including the six Nick Charles films. Their witty performances in *The Thin Man* are assisted by a well-trained fox terrier who plays Asta with an engaging lack of heroics and a healthy regard for his own skin, diving under the bed at the first sign of trouble.

Woody Van Dyke, who orchestrated the film so expertly, was a Hollywood craftsman whose 27 years of working life began under D.W. Griffith and included a number of exotic adventures in faraway places, as well as three of the five Thin Man sequels.

The Thin Man is variously reported to have been shot in 12, 14 or 16 days. Certainly it was done very quickly and a good deal of creative improvisation took place, including Nora's marvellous first entrance when she comes into the hotel laden with parcels and with Asta straining on a leash. The dog rushes to his master causing Nora and her parcels to sprawl ingloriously over the threshold. Nick looks up from chatting to his guests, glass in hand, and gestures nonchalantly towards her recumbent form as he introduces 'My wife . . . .'. This is what one finally remembers about *The Thin Man*: exchanges between two very talented performers, the speed, the fun and the wit of it. Nobody *needs* to remember who the thin man actually was.

BRENDA DAVIES

Directed by W.S. Van Dyke, 1934
Prod co: MGM. **prod**: Hunt Stromberg. **sc**: Frances Goodrich, Albert Hackett after the novel by Dashiell Hammett. **photo**: James Wong Howe. **ed**: Robert J. Kern. **art dir**: Cedric Gibbons. **cost**: Dolly Tree. **mus**: William Axt. **sd**: Douglas Shearer. **r/t**: 98 minutes.
Cast: William Powell (*Nick Charles*), Myrna Loy (*Nora Charles*), Maureen O'Sullivan (*Dorothy*), Minna Gombell (*Mimi*), Porter Hall (*MacCauley*), Henry Wadsworth (*Tommy*), William Harry (*Gilbert*), Harold Huber (*Nunheim*), Cesar Romero (*Chris*), Natalie Moorhead (*Julia Wolf*), Edward Brophy (*Morelli*), Edward Ellis (*Tynant*), Nat Pendleton (*Guild*).

Dorothy Wynant takes her new fiancé, Tommy, to meet her father – an eccentric inventor who is the 'thin man' of the title (1). A few months later, in New York, Dorothy and Tommy encounter an old friend of her father – Nick Charles (2). Newly married to the elegant, rich and witty Nora (3), Nick has retired from detective work. But, during a party where Nick is introducing his wife to his underworld contacts (4), Dorothy arrives begging Nick to find her father (5). He has disappeared after being suspected of the murder of his mistress, Julia Wolf.

Suspects include Wynant's former wife, Mimi (6 – right), her second husband Jorgensen (6 – left), and the family lawyer. Police Lieutenant Guild is baffled (7).

Summoning all those concerned to an elaborate dinner party (8 – production shot), Nick reconstructs the whole affair with such conviction that the guilty party in all three killings, Wynant's lawyer MacCauley, falls into the trap and gives himself away.

Directed by John Ford, 1939

Prod co: Walter Wanger Productions/United Artists. **exec prod:** Walter Wanger. **prod:** John Ford. **sc:** Dudley Nichols, from the story *Stage to Lordsburg* by Ernest Haycox. **photo:** Bert Glennon. **sp eff:** Ray Binger. **ed sup:** Otho Lovering. **sup:** Dorothy Spencer, Walter Reynolds. **art dir:** Alexander Toluboff, Wiard Ihnen. **cost:** Walter Plunkett. **mus:** Richard Hageman, W. Franke Harling, John Leipold, Leo Shuken, Louis Gruenberg, adapted from 17 American folk tunes of the 1880s. **mus arr:** Boris Morros. **2nd unit dir/stunts:** Yakima Canutt. **ass dir:** Wingate Smith. **r/t:** 97 minutes. **Cast:** John Wayne (*The Ringo Kid*), Claire Trevor (*Dallas*), John Carradine (*Hatfield*), Thomas Mitchell (*Dr Josiah Boone*), Andy Devine (*Buck*), Donald Meek (*Samuel Peacock*), Louise Platt (*Lucy Mallory*), Tim Holt (*Lieutenant Blanchard*), George Bancroft (*Sheriff Curly Wilcox*), Berton Churchill (*Henry Gatewood*), Tom Tyler (*Hank Plummer*), Chris Pin Martin (*Chris*), Elvira Rios (*Yakima, his wife*), Francis Ford (*Billy Pickett*), Marga Daighton (*Mrs Pickett*), Kent Odell (*Billy Pickett Jr*), Yakima Canutt (*Chief Big Tree*), Harry Tenbrook (*telegraph operator*), Jack Pennick (*Jerry, barman*), Paul McVey (*express agent*), Cornelius Keefe (*Captain Whitney*), Florence Lake (*Mrs Nancy Whitney*), Louis Mason (*sheriff*), Brenda Fowler (*Mrs Gatewood*), Walter McGrail (*Captain Sickel*), Joseph Rickson (*Luke Plummer*), Vester Pegg (*Ike Plummer*), William Hoffer (*sergeant*), Bryant Washburn (*Captain Simmons*), Nora Cecil (*Dr Boone's housekeeper*), Helen Gibson, Dorothy Annleby (*dancing girls*), Buddy Roosevelt, Bill Cody (*ranchers*), Chief White Horse (*Indian chief*), Duke Lee (*Sheriff of Lordsburg*), Mary Kathleen Walker (*Lucy's baby*).

2 WOMEN ON A DESPERATE JOURNEY WIT

NINE ODDLY ASSORTED STRANGERS start out by stagecoach for Lordsburg, New Mexico. Each has his own personal reasons for wanting to get there. Then strange things begin to happen. The telegraph is mysteriously cut... the way station burned to the ground. Danger grows steadily more menacing ... *UNTIL* ... As conventions break down, the lives of the travelers are tangled together... you live with them this strange adventure... tense, full of action... deeply moving.

STAGEC

A WALTER WANGER Production • Directed by JOHN FORD

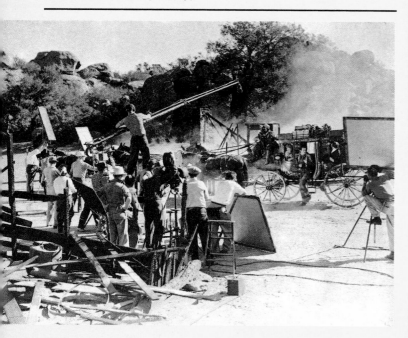

Apaches have broken out of the reservation and the telegraph wires have been cut. Nevertheless a varied group of passengers boards the stagecoach from Tonto to Lordsburg: Mrs Mallory, a pregnant wife going to join her husband, a cavalry lieutenant; Hatfield, a shady gentleman-gambler; Dallas, a prostitute run out of town by the 'decent' citizens; the bibulous and disreputable Doc Boone, who takes a keen interest in the samples carried by a timid whisky-drummer called Peacock. At the edge of the town they are joined by Gatewood, the pompous local banker. Riding alongside Buck the driver is Curly, a sheriff in pursuit of the Ringo Kid who has broken jail where he has been serving a sentence for a framed murder charge. Just outside town, Ringo himself joins the party (1). The stagecoach heads into Indian country, stopping shortly afterwards at the first staging post (2–3).

Above: John Ford – standing to the right of the boom-mike operator – filming Stagecoach

Initially, the group is strictly divided between the respectable and the disreputable, but the hazards of the journey temporarily blur the social barriers. Dallas and Doc Boone take charge of the sudden accouchement *of Mrs Mallory (4). The Ringo Kid falls in love with Dallas, who is touched by his gallantry to her. The whole party is finally united by the Indian attack (5). The cavalry charges to the rescue (6), but not before Hatfield has been killed.*

Arriving at Lordsburg, they go their different ways. The Ringo Kid avenges himself on Luke Plummer, the man who had framed him, and is reunited with Dallas. Curly, instead of arresting the Kid, connives with Doc Boone to speed the couple over the border. 'At least they're spared the blessings of civilization,' reflects the philosophic Doc.

Stagecoach has often been credited with reviving the Western in Hollywood in the Forties. Rather, though, it coincided with a whole Western boom, appearing in the same year – 1939 – as *Dodge City*, *The Oklahoma Kid*, *Union Pacific* and *Jesse James*. Even so, when Ford tried to set up the film – his first Western since *Three Bad Men* (1926) – he found the genre was badly out of fashion.

He had bought Ernest Haycox's story, which he found in *Cosmopo-*

1

RANGE MEN . . . . .

CLAIRE TREVOR • JOHN WAYNE
MITCHELL • Louise PLATT • George BANCROFT • Donald MEEK • Berton CHURCHILL • Tim HOL

litan magazine, for $2500. 'It wasn't too well developed,' he recalled, 'but the characters were good.' Producers he approached complained that people no longer went to see Westerns: 'Sure it's a Western, I said, but there are great characters

in it. What's the difference whether it's played in the West or wherever?' He took it to RKO where even the powerful Joseph P. Kennedy could not persuade his producers to adopt the project. Walter Wanger, however, who owed a film to United Artists, was finally convinced. Wanger wanted to use Gary Cooper and Marlene Dietrich for the main roles but Ford insisted that it must be cast cheaply, so he hired John Wayne – whose career had so far failed to take off, and who was making five-day Westerns – and Claire Trevor, 'a helluva actress'. Ford surrounded them with fine character players: Thomas Mitchell and Berton Churchill, both stage-trained actors; Donald Meek, George Bancroft, Andy Devine and the cadaverous John Carradine. For every one of them, the role in *Stagecoach* was to prove the most memorable of his career.

Ford himself later drew attention to the faint resemblance of the story to Maupassant's *Boule de Suif*. The critic Welford Beaton was on a better tack, however, when he described the film as 'Grand Hotel on wheels'. The essence of the story is the interaction of a little group of characters under the stress of a perilous journey.

The structure of the film is very formal. It divides neatly into eight carefully balanced episodes, of which the central and longest is the 24-minute sequence at the Apache Wells staging post with the birth of Mrs Mallory's baby, and the climax is the six and a half minutes of the Indian attack. The expository opening scene, set in Tonto, lasts 12 minutes, during which time every character is carefully and comprehensively introduced.

The characters are also exactly balanced; in one group are the respectable' people – Hatfield, Gatewood (actually an embezzler) and Mrs Mallory; in the other, the 'disreputables' – the Ringo Kid, Doc Boone and Dallas. Buck and Curly, outside the coach, stand aside, a sort of chorus upon the moral debate waged within the coach. The mild little whisky-drummer, too, has a detached function. It is he who states the simple moral of the film: 'Let us have a little Christian charity, one to another.'

The picture was made for $222,000 – $8000 under the assigned budget. The scenes in Monument Valley were completed in four days; the rest was shot on the Goldwyn lot. The Monument Valley days included the extraordinary stunt material staged by Yakima Canutt. Canutt related that after he had performed his most hair-raising feat – jumping onto the stagecoach's lead horse and then, in response to Ringo's rifle shots, falling first to the shafts and then to the ground, allowing six horses and the stage to drive over his prone body – he ran to Ford to ask if the cameras had caught it. 'Even if they didn't,' said Ford, 'I'll not shoot that again.'

At that time there were no specifically equipped camera cars, and ordinary automobiles were used for the amazing scenes where the cameras follow the chase at full speed. The cameramen found to their surprise that in keeping up

with the horses they were driving at 40–42 miles per hour.

'I shot it pretty much as it is written,' said Ford, though Dudley Nichols was on the set throughout the film to write – or more likely to cut – dialogue as required. What is striking is the economy of the script. A broken half-line or two will often brilliantly illuminate a character or a situation. At the end, when the characters are returning to their own worlds, Mrs Mallory makes a hopeless attempt to prolong the brief contact with Dallas. 'If there is ever anything …' she begins awkwardly; 'I know,' says Dallas, understanding, but decisively acknowledging the unbridgeable gulf between them in the hypocritical, rigid society of their times.

Stagecoach stands alone for the epic quality both of its panoramas of the West and its human emotions. At the same time it permanently formed Western style. Ford was the first to make use of the spectacular topography of Monument Valley, and was to return to it many times again himself. The final shoot-out, which he had already used in silent films, and was to use again in *My Darling Clementine* (1946), has, since *Stagecoach*, become a cliché.

'It went back to what Wyatt Earp had told me. Wyatt was a friend of mine – in fact I still have his rifle in the corner of my bedroom.'

Ford has always stayed this close to his own West.

DAVID ROBINSON

3

4

5

6

HUMPHREY BOGART
MARY ASTOR
THE Maltese Falcon

by DASHIELL HAMMETT *Author of* THE THIN MAN

1

4

The Maltese Falcon regularly attracts the accolade – rarely disputed – of the best thriller ever made. It is a prototype of the Forties *film noir*, a model of movie narrative; and in the short term it launched a whole series of pictures with Peter Lorre and Sydney Greenstreet as a kind of Laurel and Hardy of crime.

It was John Huston's first assignment as a director, the reward of ten years' outstanding work as a scenarist at Warner Brothers, during which time he had collaborated on a notable run of scripts including *Murders in the Rue Morgue* (1932), *The Amazing Dr Clitterhouse*, *Jezebel* (both 1938), *Juarez* (1939), *Dr Ehrlich's Magic Bullet* (1940) and *High Sierra* (1941), in which Humphrey Bogart had his first real starring role.

Huston – in his early years a soldier, bum, boxer, playboy, ham and writer by turns – could hardly fail to be sympathetic to the author of the original novel. Dashiell Hammett had left school at thirteen and had been a newsboy, freight-clerk, stevedore, advertising manager and Pinkerton Detective (he worked on the Fatty Arbuckle case) before turning to writing when struck by tuberculosis. As a novelist he revealed, through the improbable medium of pulp detective stories, a major literary talent.

The Maltese Falcon provided Huston with a theme that was often to recur in his subsequent films: a motley and dubious group of characters in passionate search of a treasure that, in the outcome, proved illusory. (It had been a popular literary theme at least as far back as Chaucer's *Pardoner's Tale*.)

Hammett's *The Maltese Falcon* had already been filmed twice before: in 1931 by Roy del Ruth, with

Directed by John Huston, 1941
Prod co: Warner Brothers. **prod**: Hal Wallis. **sc**: John Huston, from the book by Dashiell Hammett. **photo**: Arthur Edison. **ed**: Thomas Richards. **mus**: Adolph Deutsch. **mus dir**: Leo F. Forbstein. **r/t**: 100 minutes.
Cast: Humphrey Bogart (*Sam Spade*), Mary Astor (*Brigid O'Shaughnessy*), Sydney Greenstreet (*Kasper Gutman*), Peter Lorre (*Joel Cairo*), Elisha Cook Jr (*Wilmer Cook*), Gladys George (*Iva Archer*), Barton MacLane (*Lt of Detectives Dundy*), Ward Bond (*Detective Tom Polhaus*), Walter Huston (*Captain Jacobi*), Jerome Cowan (*Miles Archer*).

Bebe Daniels and Ricardo Cortez, and in 1936, as *Satan Met a Lady*, by William Dieterle, with Bette Davies and Warren Williams. Only Huston's version is now remembered.

George Raft had been offered the role of Sam Spade, but the actor was not prepared to risk his reputation with a new director; so Huston accepted Bogart instead. (In *High Sierra*, too, Bogart had succeeded to a role rejected by Raft.) Bogart had had a decade of gangster roles – in his first 34 pictures for Warners he was a jailbird in nine, electrocuted or hung in eight, and riddled by bullets in thirteen. *The Maltese Falcon* released him from this role and established his lasting image as the sardonic, romantic private detective, operating in a shadowy and seedy world of urban crime, thus launching the major period of his career.

One of Huston's later dicta was 'The trick is in the casting' and *The Maltese Falcon* proved this. Mary Astor, already 35, with twenty years of films behind her and near the end of her starring career, was cast as Brigid. She brought her great intelligence to the role:

'She was a congenital liar ("I am a liar. I've always been a liar") and slightly psychopathic. And that kind of liar wears the face of truth, although they send out all sorts of signals that they are lying... One of the tip-offs is that they can't help

5

A beautiful woman walks into the office of Spade and Archer (1), private investigators, with an assignment to follow a man, Floyd Thursby, whom she alleges (not very convincingly) has eloped with her sister. That night, Miles Archer, tailing Floyd Thursby, is shot dead. So, a few hours later, is Thursby. Sam Spade investigating the murders, is fascinated and attracted by the beautiful client (2) even though her mendacity extends to grave uncertainty over her name, which *may* be Brigid O'Shaughnessy.

Brigid proves to be one of a mixed group of shady characters: the others are the effeminate Joel Cairo (3), Wilmur, a dim-witted young hood (4), and Gutman, the 'fat man' (5) – all in pursuit of a priceless antique; a jewelled falcon that once belonged to the Knights of St John of Malta. After complex deceits, counter-deceits, violence and murder, Sam Spade comes into possession of the Falcon (6). The machinations and the bargaining all prove fruitless when the bird turns out to be a fake (7). Realizing that it was Brigid who killed Thursby, Spade, with mixed emotions, hands her over to the police detectives Dundy and Polhaus (8), along with the rest of the gang.

2

3

breathing rather rapidly. So, I hyperventilated before going into most of the scenes. It gave me a heady feeling of thinking at cross purposes . . .'

The Hungarian-born Peter Lorre had been a favourite character actor in both America and Britain since his flight from Nazi Germany. Sydney Greenstreet had – after a brief period as a Ceylon tea planter in his youth – spent a lifetime as a stage actor. This was his first film, and at 62 he approached it nervously. The first scene he had to shoot was the demanding sequence in which Gutman spins out the history of the Maltese Falcon while anxiously watching Spade for the effects of the drugs he has given him.

Walter Huston, the director's father, made an uncredited appearance as the seaman who staggers into Spade's office with the Falcon and then drops down dead. The

elder Huston complained that this short scene demanded not only a whole day's work but left him black and blue from twenty takes and twenty falls.

However so many takes were exceptional. Huston had precisely scripted and pre-planned the film, the work went quickly and effectively with no changes or improvisations on the set, and The Maltese Falcon was brought in well under budget. Mary Astor recalls that on one occasion the complicated shot scheduled for a day was finished in seven minutes and two takes and the company spent the rest of the day at the pool. The picture was largely filmed in sequence, which relieved the company's general confusion about the complex plot – in which all the loose ends are, nevertheless, very neatly caught up by the end of the film.

Already Huston's self-effacing style was clear. The camerawork

has been appreciatively described by the critic (and later writer of The African Queen, 1951) James Agee:

'Much that is best in Huston's work comes of his sense of what is natural to the eye and his delicate, simple feeling for space relationships: his camera huddles close to those who huddle to talk, leans back a proportionate distance, relaxing, if they talk casually. He hates camera rhetoric and the shot-for-shot's sake; but because he takes each moment catch-as-catch-can and is so deeply absorbed in doing the best possible thing with it, he has made any number of unforgettable shots.'

It is perhaps that readiness in Huston to use methods not because they are orthodox, or modish, but because they are *right*, which gives his most memorable films the quality of always improving with time, rather than dating.

DAVID ROBINSON

7

8

Directed by Michael Curtiz, 1942
Prod co: Warner Brothers/First National. **prod:** Hal B. Wallis. **sc:** Julius J. Epstein, Philip G. Epstein, Howard Koch, from the play *Everybody Goes to Rick's* by Murray Burnett, Joan Alison. **photo:** Arthur Edeson. **ed:** Owen Marks. **montage sequence:** Don Siegel, James Leicester. **art dir:** Carl Jules Weyl. **mus dir:** Leo F. Forbstein. **mus:** Max Steiner. **songs:** 'As Time Goes By' by Herman Hopfeld, 'Knock on Wood' by M. K. Jerome, Jack Scholl. **ass dir:** Lee Katz. **narr:** Lou Marcelle. **r/t:** 102 mins.
Cast: Humphrey Bogart (*Rick*), Ingrid Bergman (*Ilsa*), Paul Henreid (*Victor Laszlo*), Claude Rains (*Captain Louis Renault*), Conrad Veidt (*Major Strasser*), Sydney Greenstreet (*Señor Ferrari*), Peter Lorre (*Ugarte*), S. Z. Sakall (*Carl*), Madelaine LeBeau (*Yvonne*), Dooley Wilson (*Sam*), Joy Page (*Annina Brandel*), John Qualen (*Berger*), Leonid Kinsky (*Sascha*), Helmut Dantine (*Jan Brandel*), Curt Bois (*pickpocket*), Marcel Dalio (*croupier*), Corinna Mura (*singer*), Ludwig Stossel (*Mr Leuchtag*), Ilka Gruning (*Mrs Leuchtag*), Charles La Torre (*Italian officer Tonelli*), Frank Puglia (*Arab vendor*), Dan Seymour (*Abdul*).

Casablanca is, simply, *the* 'cult' film. A commercial hit when released, and the winner of three Oscars, the film has increased in popularity over the last four decades so that few filmgoers in the Western world have not seen it at least once. The reasons for the film's continuing popularity include various levels of nostalgia, although that alone is an insufficient explanation. Other, perhaps more important, reasons are to be found in the film itself which remains surprisingly contemporary in spite of its specific setting in time.

First of all there is that nostalgia – even in contemporary audiences – for the sort of film *Casablanca* is: the well-made, fast-moving, big studio collaborative melodrama. Various proponents of the *auteur* theory have claimed that the credit

for the film's quality should go to the director or to the script – and certainly both deserve the highest praise – but the film would hardly be what it is without Warner Brothers' specific production team and policies. The former accounts for such things as the atmospheric lighting and sets; the latter for the breakneck speed with which the complicated story is told without one wasted frame. The script is witty, sophisticated, well-structured and tight, but hardly a 'personal statement' by the scriptwriters, particularly considering that the ending was written and shot in at least two versions before the studio decided which would be used. Even with that script and director, would *Casablanca* still be watched had the originally planned cast been used? Ronald Reagan, Ann Sheridan and

Dennis Morgan are hardly Bogart, Bergman and Henreid. Nor would it have had the same colouration and humour without the Warner repertory company: from Claude Rains, Sydney Greenstreet and Peter Lorre, down to Helmut Dantine and Dan Seymour.

The Bogart image, the 'existentialist hero', began taking shape in 1941 with *High Sierra* and *The Maltese Falcon*, but was completed by *Casablanca* which has become the central film for the Bogart 'cult'. One of the walking wounded, his earlier idealism and romanticism having turned into a belief only in his own code of ethics, a rejection of sham, and an ability to turn his

back on 'romantic love', Bogart remains a hero for our times.

There is a nostalgic element in the film itself, one which cannot help but appeal to modern audiences. The world seemed simpler for Rick and Ilsa before the Germans marched into Paris and tore apart all of their romantic illusions. The Casablanca of the film is a microcosm of the world turned upside down by the war: bankers have become pastry cooks and everything held sacred before is now to be bartered for exit visas and survival. Ilsa says 'With the whole world crumbling, we pick this time to fall in love.' The world is still crumbling, and the film's approach to that,

2

3

6

In December of 1941 refugees of every description find themselves in Casablanca trying desperately to obtain visas to freedom. Most find their way to Rick's Café Américain (1), run by Richard Blaine, a disillusioned former soldier of fortune. He refuses to save a small-time crook, Ugarte (2), who is shot by the Vichy police after he has given Rick two invaluable letters of transit for safekeeping. Moments later Victor Laszlo, a leader of the European underground, and his wife Ilsa arrive. Ilsa and Rick were lovers in pre-Occupation Paris (3), but she left him suddenly when she learned that her husband was still alive. She visits Rick that night, but he is bitter and unforgiving towards her (4).

The Laszlos desperately need to escape the Nazis – particularly Major Strasser (5) who is determined that they will not leave Casablanca. They approach the black-market boss, Señor Ferrari (6), in the hope of buying visas, and he advises them to go to Rick, whom he suspects of hiding the letters of transit, but Rick ungraciously refuses to help them. That night Ilsa visits him secretly while her husband is at an Underground meeting. She threatens to shoot him, but finally breaks down and explains why she had to desert him in Paris. She wants to stay with him, and he allows her to think that he will give the documents to Laszlo.

Rick leads Captain Renault, the prefect of police, to believe that he and Ilsa are going to leave Casablanca together, and arranges to have Laszlo arrested in the Café. But he double-crosses Renault and forces him to take them to the airport (7). Ilsa leaves reluctantly with her husband, realizing that his work is more important than her love for Rick.

When Major Strasser arrives, having been warned of the escape by the cunning Renault, Rick kills him (8) and Renault tells his men to 'round up the usual suspects'. He and Rick walk off into the night, with Rick declaring '. . . this is the beginning of a beautiful friendship'.

sardonic and cynical yet idealistic and resistant, makes *Casablanca* entirely relevant today.

Given the fact that one of the aims of the film was to rouse America from its isolationism (irrelevant, finally, as the Japanese bombing of Pearl Harbor happened before the film's release), it is a moot point as to how many of the film's ambiguities were intentional. It is difficult to know if the film's original audiences found Ilsa and her husband Laszlo as one dimensional and as ultimately boring as do modern audiences. Laszlo, for all his 'courage', has no personality apart from 'the cause'. Ilsa, for all the misty close-ups of the Bergman charms, is a walking romantic cliché – lines such as 'Was that cannon fire – or is my heart pounding?' exactly delineate Ilsa's character. Her horrendous insistence on the wonders of self-sacrifice are unsuited to the zip, the toughness, and the clarity of Rick and Captain Renault. It is no wonder Rick chooses the humorous and understanding friendship of the latter over the tears and clunking idealism of the former.

Perhaps nostalgia is not what it used to be, but with *Casablanca* it surely is, especially when audiences come to see the film in order to re-experience the past and are left facing their present.

DAVID OVERBEY

7

8

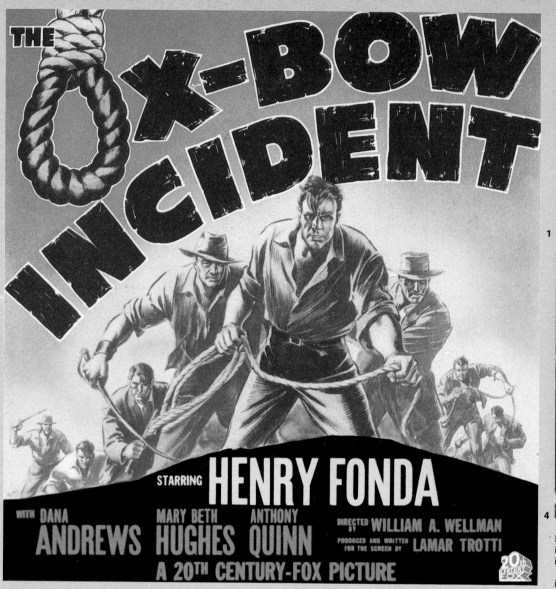

THE OX-BOW INCIDENT

STARRING HENRY FONDA

WITH DANA **ANDREWS** MARY BETH **HUGHES** ANTHONY **QUINN**

DIRECTED BY **WILLIAM A. WELLMAN**

PRODUCED AND WRITTEN FOR THE SCREEN BY **LAMAR TROTTI**

A 20TH CENTURY-FOX PICTURE

1

4

Directed by William A. Wellman, 1943
Prod co: 20th Century-Fox. **exec prod:** Darryl F. Zanuck. **prod:** Lamarr Trotti. **sc:** Lamarr Trotti, from the novel by Walter Van Tilburg Clark. **photo:** Arthur Miller. **ed:** Allen McNeil. **art dir:** Richard Day, James Basevi. **mus:** Cyril J. Mockridge. **r/t:** 77 minutes. Released in GB as *Strange Incident*.
Cast: Henry Fonda (*Gil Carter*), Dana Andrews (*Martin*), Mary Beth Hughes (*Rose Mapen*), Anthony Quinn (*Mexican*), William Eythe (*Gerald*), Henry Morgan (*Art Croft*), Jane Darwell (*Ma Grier*), Matt Briggs (*Judge Daniel Tyler*), Harry Davenport (*Arthur Davies*), Frank Conroy (*Major Tetley*), Marc Lawrence (*Reverend Farnley*), Francis Ford ('*Dad*'), George Chandler (*stage driver*)

William Wellman's celebrated polemic against lynch law has arbitrarily been described as the first 'psychological' Western. The claim is as dubious as it is vague, since at least two earlier examples of the genre, *White Gold* (dir. William K. Howard, 1927) and *The Wind* (dir. Victor Sjöström, 1928), have been similarly cited.

The Ox-Bow Incident's true significance lies in the fact that it was the first Western of any importance to deal uncompromisingly and in a literate manner with a social issue, forsaking completely the escapist trappings, heroism, high idealism and black-and-white morality of the traditional Western. It was also the first to delve deeply into the minds and motives of a variety of realistic characters confronted with a situation completely outside their normal experience.

More aptly, some commentators have called Wellman's film the first 'anti-Western', i.e. a social drama which exploits the Western formula to criticize modern social evils. As such it did indeed presage a new trend in the Western form, heralding the strain of introspective Westerns of the Forties and Fifties – which included Raoul Walsh's *Pursued* (1947) and *Colorado Territory* (1949), Wellman's own *Yellow Sky* (1948), John Sturges' *The Capture* (1950) and, most notably, Henry King's *The Gunfighter* (1950) and Fred Zinnemann's classic, *High Noon* (1952).

The Ox-Bow Incident's closest antecedent was Fritz Lang's condemnation of bigotry and mob violence, *Fury* (1936), although Wellman himself had already rehearsed the lynching theme in his 1932 film, *The Conquerors*, in a scene regarded by Western historian William K. Everson as:

'. . . so starkly designed and lit, and so casually under-played, that it quite outshines the more carefully and lengthily constructed lynching scenes in . . . *The Ox-Bow Incident*.'

Lynching had of course occurred as a theme in other, earlier Westerns, such as *The Virginian* (dir. Victor Fleming, 1929), in which the hero (Gary Cooper) supervises the hanging of his best friend for stealing cattle. The difference, as exemplified by *Fury* and *The Ox-Bow Incident*, is that a decade of rapidly growing social consciousness in America had turned the act from one of barely questioned rough justice into something that was abhorrent to a civilized society. This is further emphasized in *The Ox-Bow Incident* by the fact that, despite the sympathetic presence of Henry Fonda, the film has no hero in the conventional sense. As Robert Warshow points out in his essay *The Westerner*:

'. . . a hero would have to stop the lynching or be killed in trying to stop it, and then the "problem" of lynching would no longer be central.'

In other words, every participant in the hanging in *The Ox-Bow Incident* is to blame, whether he or she approves of the deed or not.

In making the film, Wellman and his scriptwriter Lamarr Trotti (who also scripted *Yellow Sky*) remained as faithful as possible to the original novel by Walter Van Tilburg Clark. Wellman felt strongly enough about the project to have purchased the rights to the book himself. He spent many months touting it round the studios before Darryl F. Zanuck accepted the property for 20th Century-Fox. Zanuck undoubtedly recognized that it would fail at the box-office, being totally out of key with the escapist fantasies and optimistic, patriotic dramas which were then the almost-exclusive wartime fare, but perhaps saw its worth in terms of the prestige the film would bring to the studio.

The timing of the production had a crucial effect on the final script. Despite its general fidelity to Clark's book, the screenplay ultimately shied away from the novel's utter pessimism and total condemnation of human fallibility. Many commentators have pointed out how the film softens and sentimentalizes Clark's harsh message (notably in Fonda's reading of the letter written by the victimized Martin, which does not occur in the book), and offers humankind's conscience

14

The scene is Nevada in 1885. The men of Bridger's Wells are roused to hatred and revenge when they learn that a local rancher, Kincaid, has been murdered by cattle rustlers. With the sheriff out of town, the townsfolk raise a posse (1), despite protests by one of them, Arthur Davies, that their action is illegal. Gil Carter and Art Croft, two riders passing through, reluctantly agree to join the manhunt to prevent suspicion falling on them (2).

The posse comes upon three men – an old half-wit, a Mexican and their leader, Martin (3). Martin claims to have bought cattle from Kincaid to stock a derelict ranch, but has no bill of sale to back up his story.

Although he protests their innocence, the three are condemned to be summarily hanged (4).

Some support is aroused for the accused men, but a sadistic ex-Confederate officer, Major Tetley, makes an eloquent case for the lynching (5). With only seven of the mob voting to await the sheriff's return, the men are hanged from a tree (6, 7).

Too late, the sheriff arrives with word that Kincaid is not dead, only hurt, and that the real culprits have been apprehended. The mob disperses in shame, Tetley commits suicide and, back in the saloon, Gil Carter reads aloud a letter written by Martin to his wife (8). He then rides out with Art to deliver it.

a ray of hope where Clark gives none. But in Wellman's defence, it has to be noted that an American audience could hardly have been expected to swallow an implicit indictment of itself as inherently evil at a time when it was battling against evil incarnate in the shape of German and Japanese fascism.

Another criticism levelled at The Ox-Bow Incident is its preponderant use of studio 'exteriors' and the resultant artificiality these give to the film's appearance. But apart from their practicality in allowing Wellman to control his night-scene

lighting, it may be equally argued that the studio sets enhance the nightmarish atmosphere of the film and lend to the central scenes an apt expressionistic quality.

Aside from these points, what is important about The Ox-Bow Incident is that, in its modest 77 minutes, it irrevocably altered the nature of the Western, remaining one of the few qualified to support to the full the director Sam Peckinpah's assertion that 'the Western is a universal frame within which it is possible to comment on today'.
CLYDE JEAVONS

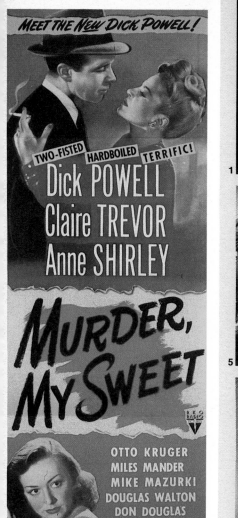

MEET THE *NEW* DICK POWELL!

TWO-FISTED HARDBOILED TERRIFIC!

Dick POWELL
Claire TREVOR
Anne SHIRLEY

MURDER, MY SWEET

RKO RADIO

OTTO KRUGER
MILES MANDER
MIKE MAZURKI
DOUGLAS WALTON
DON DOUGLAS

Produced by Adrian Scott • Directed by Edward Dmytryk
Screen Play by John Paxton

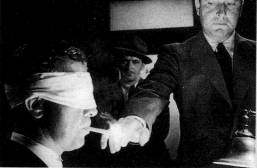

1

2

5

6

9

10

Directed by Edward Dmytryk, 1944

Prod co: RKO. **prod:** Adrian Scott. **exec prod:** Sid Rogell. **sc:** John Paxton, from the novel *Farewell, My Lovely* by Raymond Chandler. **photo:** Harry J. Wild. **sp eff:** Vernon L. Walker, Douglas Trower. **ed:** Joseph Noriega. **art dir:** Albert S. D'Agostino, Carroll Clark, Darrell Silvera, Michael Ohrenbach. **mus:** Roy Webb. **mus dir:** C. Bakaleinikoff. **sd:** Bailey Fesler. **ass dir:** William Dorfman, Leslie Urbach. **r/t:** 95 minutes. Released in GB as *Farewell, My Lovely*.
Cast: Dick Powell (*Philip Marlowe*), Claire Trevor (*Mrs Grayle*), Anne Shirley (*Ann Grayle*), Otto Kruger (*Jules Amthor*), Mike Mazurki (*Moose Malloy*), Douglas Walton (*Lindsay Marriott*), Miles Mander (*Mr Grayle*), Don Douglas (*Lt Randall*), Ralf Harolde (*Dr Sonderborg*), Esther Howard (*Mrs Florian*).

Police question private detective Philip Marlowe about his possible complicity in a multiple murder (1). Marlow recounts the events leading up to the killings . . .

An ex-convict, Moose Malloy, hires Marlowe to find Velma, his former girlfriend (2). Moose takes Marlowe to Florian's bar where Velma used to work, but she has long since left. Marlowe traces the bar's former owner, Mrs Florian, who reluctantly parts with a photograph of Velma (3).

Marlowe is later hired by a socialite, Lindsay Marriott. Marriott claims he has been asked by a friend, Mrs Grayle, to buy back an irreplaceable jade necklace from the crooks who

stole it. Marlowe drives Marriott to the rendezvous (4) and is then knocked unconscious. When he comes to, he finds Marriott dead. Later he encounters Ann Grayle, Mrs Grayle's stepdaughter, who offers him money to give up the case; although attracted by her, he refuses.

Mrs Grayle, the sexy wife of a rich, elderly man, hires Marlowe to find Marriott's killer (5), suggesting that Jules Amthor, who runs a private sanatorium, may be implicated. Amthor, meanwhile, has convinced Moose that Marlowe is concealing Velma's whereabouts. Moose kidnaps Marlowe and hands him over to Amthor (6). Marlowe is

drugged by one of Amthor's associates (7) but manages to escape.

At her beach house, Mrs Grayle tells Marlowe that she is being blackmailed by Amthor (8) and asks Marlowe to bring him to the beach house. Marlowe goes to see him but finds him dead, the victim of Moose's rage. Marlowe tells Moose that he will take him to Velma.

Leaving Moose outside the beach house, Marlowe tells Mrs Grayle that Amthor will presently be joining them. Mrs Grayle offers Marlowe the supposedly stolen necklace as a reward. He refuses to let himself be drawn into her double-dealings and then accuses her of killing Marriott. As Mrs Grayle is about to shoot Marlowe (9), Ann and her father arrive. Appalled by his wife's murderous scheming, Grayle shoots her (10). Moose then bursts in (11), recognizes the dead woman as his long-lost Velma and turns on Mr Grayle, who is forced to kill him (12); Marlowe is temporarily blinded by the gunfire (13) – hence the bandages. After recounting this story to the police Marlowe leaves with Ann Grayle (14).

Edward Dmytryk's *Murder, My Sweet* was the second screen version of the Raymond Chandler novel which, two years earlier, had rather humiliatingly done service at RKO as the basis of *The Falcon Takes Over*, one of the Falcon series of B pictures. In 1975, a third version was filmed, directed by Dick Richards and starring Robert Mitchum.

The basic reason behind the property's promotion from B material in 1942 to the substance of an A feature two years later are not hard to find. By 1944 *film noir* was in vogue; that year alone saw the release of such movies as *Laura*, *The Woman in the Window* and *Double Indemnity* (the last-named co-scripted by Chandler himself). All these films are crime melodramas that turn – as does *Murder, My Sweet* – on the notion of the *femme fatale*.

A further prevailing characteristic is an elaborate structure and time-scale (doubtless traceable to the influence of *Citizen Kane*, 1940). Unlike Chandler's novel, which proceeds chronologically, John Paxton's screenplay is constructed as a flashback from what is ultimately revealed to be the story's finishing point as Marlowe attempts to explain himself to the police.

In keeping with the atmosphere of paranoia that characterizes *film noir*, the movie's narrative follows a circular pattern and also constitutes a struggle towards elucidation. A particularly pleasing conceit in this regard is that because Marlowe has (it transpires) been temporarily blinded by powder burns in the climactic shoot-out, he is blind-folded by bandages in the sequences that frame the main story. It is fair to add, of course, that the film is sufficiently conventional to wind up with a statutory romantic fade-out, reuniting Marlowe with the somewhat arbitrarily introduced love interest represented by Ann Grayle.

All the same, the world the film occupies is a dark one in every sense, with virtually every sequence taking place at night, whether the setting be the foggy canyon where Marlowe is set upon by an anonymous assailant or the placid residential street into which he staggers after escaping from the phoney sanatorium.

And not only is this a world of night, it is also one of phantasmagoria. Nowhere is this hallucinatory visual dimension more memorable than in the introduction of the hulking Moose as a reflection on the window of Marlowe's office, which itself opens onto a threatening vista of the nocturnal city.

More debatable, perhaps, is the use of optical superimpositions to duplicate Marlowe's sensations of being knocked out and drugged; but while these now undeniably date the film, it must be conceded that they have a nightmarish aptness and that they duplicate the more overwrought tendencies of Chandler's prose.

Nor do they impede the narrative pace, for Paxton succeeded admirably in translating a complicated plot into dramatic action, improving in some respects on his source material, particularly in the compression of the finale.

But however smoothly *Murder, My Sweet* purrs along beneath its *film noir* styling, thanks to its finely tuned narrative and the calibre of its supporting players (especially Claire Trevor as the vengeful, duplicitous woman of mystery), it still depends crucially upon the presence of Dick Powell as Marlowe.

Powell's standing in the role has been eclipsed by the cult of Humphrey Bogart, who, playing Marlowe in *The Big Sleep* two years later, virtually absorbed the character into his own screen personality. At the time, of course, Powell was demonstrably cast against type: the baby-faced star of the Busby Berkeley musicals hardly seemed to have the makings of a hard-boiled detective. Yet the knowingness of Powell's early persona provided the basis for a highly effective transformation. His Marlowe possesses a rough-diamond edge – consonant with a greater emphasis on the character's money-grubbing instincts than later adaptations would allow – which throws into relief rather than sub-

dues the sympathetic qualities of Chandler's creation.

Writing about the film on its first appearance in Britain, Dilys Powell spoke with her matchlessly elegant precision of its exactly achieving Chandler's 'peculiar mixture of harshness, sensuality, high polish and backstreet poetry'. It is thanks to Dick Powell's playing as much as to the high-quality RKO craftsmanship at Dmytryk's command that, after all these years, the mixture so distinctively retains its headiness.

TIM PULLEINE

Right: in Britain the film retained the title of Chandler's novel

3

7

11

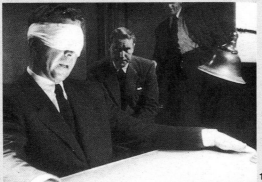

13

8

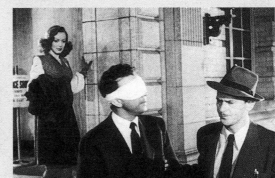

12

14

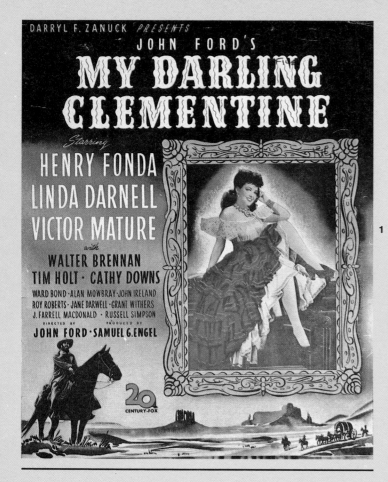

DARRYL F. ZANUCK *PRESENTS*

JOHN FORD'S
MY DARLING CLEMENTINE

Starring

HENRY FONDA
LINDA DARNELL
VICTOR MATURE

with

WALTER BRENNAN
TIM HOLT · CATHY DOWNS

WARD BOND · ALAN MOWBRAY · JOHN IRELAND
ROY ROBERTS · JANE DARWELL · GRANT WITHERS
J. FARRELL MACDONALD · RUSSELL SIMPSON

DIRECTED BY   PRODUCED BY
JOHN FORD · SAMUEL G. ENGEL

20 CENTURY-FOX

1

2

Directed by John Ford, 1946
Prod co: 20th Century-Fox. **prod:** Samuel G. Engel. **sc:** Samuel G. Engel, Winston Miller, from a story by Sam Hellman based on the book *Wyatt Earp, Frontier Marshal* by Stuart N. Lake. **photo:** Joseph P. MacDonald. **ed:** Dorothy Spencer. **art dir:** James Basevi, Lyle Wheeler, Thomas Little, Fred J. Rode. **cost:** Rene Hubert. **mus:** Cyril J. Mockridge. **ass dir:** William Eckhardt. **r/t:** 97 minutes.
Cast: Henry Fonda (*Wyatt Earp*), Linda Darnell (*Chihuahua*), Victor Mature (*Doc Holliday*), Walter Brennan (*Old Man Clanton*), Tim Holt (*Virgil Earp*), Ward Bond (*Morgan Earp*), Cathy Downs (*Clementine Carter*), Alan Mowbray (*Granville Thorndyke*), John Ireland (*Billy Clanton*), Grant Withers (*Ike Clanton*), Roy Roberts (*mayor*), Jane Darwell (*Kate Nelson*), Russell Simpson (*John Simpson*), Francis Ford (*Dad*), J. Farrell MacDonald (*Mac*), Don Garner (*James Earp*), Ben Hall (*barber*), Mickey Simpson (*Sam Clanton*), Fred Libby (*Phin Clanton*), Charles Stevens (*Indian*), Arthur Walsh (*hotel clerk*), Jack Pennick (*stage driver*), Louis Mercier (*François*), Harry Woods (*Luke*).

The gunfight at the OK Corral, Tombstone, Arizona on October 26, 1881, was without doubt one of the most famous events in the history of the American West. It is hardly surprising that John Ford – of all great American film directors the one to show consistently a passion for his country's history – should include it in one of his finest Westerns, *My Darling Clementine*.

Right up to the last moments of the film, when the shoot-out takes place, it is impossible to foresee what is going to happen because the director has managed to portray the central character Wyatt Earp not as the legendary figure that the real gunfight made him, but as an ordinary human being going about his day-to-day activities. In *My Darling Clementine* Wyatt the man is constantly given precedence over Wyatt the hero. The film has none of the usual elements of the Wyatt Earp 'myths' or any vindication of the

triumph of law over the anarchy and violence of the Old West. However, this frees the spectator to draw conclusions that are never explicitly stated and which gain in strength from this apparent indifference. As events unfold on the screen, moral certitude becomes so absolute that Ford is even able to use an audacious ellipsis in the culminating moment of the gunfight: the death of Old Man Clanton takes place off screen, as though the director were only concerned with the eradication of evil in order to be able to release his central character for other adventures.

Whatever the circumstances, Wyatt behaves with dignity and restraint. He is a man who loves peace and tranquility and only accepts a more dynamic role when driven by the brutal killing of his younger brother and the theft of his livestock. In contrast there is Doc Holliday, one of Ford's least

characteristic anti-heroes. Always dressed in black, he is a dandy fascinated by risk, whose search for the absolute has unaccountably led him to a slow and systematic destruction of his talents. He has given up being a doctor and left his fiancée Clementine in order to take refuge in Tombstone. Haunted by the thought of a death that he knows to be close at hand, but still more terrified of braving life, he repeatedly tries to provoke a confrontation that would be fatal to him. Suicidal, identifying himself with Hamlet's agony, uprooted and out of place in this primitive West to which he introduces an element of absurdity and nihilism, Doc Holliday is the complete opposite to Wyatt Earp. In the eyes of civilization he is the man without motive, the poet and the vagabond.

Ford was indisputably one of the cinema's most skilful portrayers of American family life, which he regarded as the institution central to collective living and a reservoir of stable values. It is significant that *My Darling Clementine* begins as a family drama – with the killing of James Earp turning Wyatt and his brothers against the Clanton family. These two clans are also led into conflict by their different ways of life. The Earps are a united family that extends its community-mindedness to their cleaning up of Tombstone and whose profound sense of interdependence even transcends death. On the other hand there are the Clantons, symbolically isolated in the heart of the wild country, pillaging and leading a life as primitive as it is violent. They are dominated by a threaten-

Below: Henry Fonda, John Ford and Cathy Downs on the set of My Darling Clementine

ing father-figure who disobeys the law and rules his sons with fear.

While the Clantons are only united in a violence that alienates them from the community, the Earps merge more and more into the large 'family' of Tombstone, joining in the ceremonies – the church service and the dance – that mark the bringing of peace to the township.

These rituals also bring together a man and a woman, Wyatt and Clementine, and allow them to express their unspoken feelings for each other. Their timid and repressed love is the counterpart of the more tragic love of Doc for Clementine and the sincere but fated love of Chihuahua for Doc. Throughout the film each character pursues another who denies him and continues along the path that he (or she) has carved out for himself. Doc fulfils his destiny and Chihuahua pays for her lie about the medallion, both by dying; Clementine – who comes from the East bringing civilization – stays on in Tombstone as a teacher; and Wyatt finally finds his vocation as a cowboy and decides to take to the trail again.

The last scene of the film could well be Ford's trade mark: a woman stands watching a man disappearing along a road, his lust for adventure not yet satisfied. For Wyatt, the episode in Tombstone was only a stage in his migration, an interval in which he tasted the 'charms' of a civilization for which he does not feel the need for any permanent attachment; at the end he rejoins the majestic scenery of Monument Valley where the first events of the story took place. It is a scenery forever inhabited by the vast family of Ford's heroes and Wyatt goes back to them with regular, peaceful footsteps.   OLIVIER EYQUEM

18

3

4

5

6

7

8

Driving their cattle west, Wyatt Earp (1) and his brothers make camp outside Tombstone. While Wyatt, Morgan and Virgil are in town, James is shot dead and the herd stolen. Wyatt agrees to become marshal and confronts the Clantons with the murder of his brother (2).

After dumping saloon-girl Chihuahua in a horse trough for spying on his poker hand (3), Wyatt is challenged by her man, gunslinger Doc Holliday (4). But instead of fighting, the two become friends. Pretty Clementine Carter, who was Doc's nurse in his old practice, arrives in town (5) to persuade him to go back East with her, but he refuses and gets drunk. Wyatt takes Clementine to Tombstone's first ever church service and to a celebratory dance (6).

Doc leaves town on his own. Chihuahua blames Clementine and they fight. When Wyatt separates them, he sees that Chihuahua is wearing a medallion (7) taken from James when he was killed. She tells him Doc gave it to her and Wyatt rides after him, wounds him (8) and brings him back. Billy Clanton shoots down Chihuahua (9) when she confesses that it was he who gave her the medallion. Wyatt's shot hits him but he escapes and is pursued by Virgil. Doc prepares to operate on Chihuahua (10). Billy dies and Old Man Clanton kills Virgil. Wyatt finds his body on the street.

Wyatt and Morgan go to the OK Corral for a final showdown with the Clantons (11). Chihuahua has died and Doc joins the Earps. In the shoot-out the Clantons and Doc (12) are killed. Wyatt and Morgan leave Tombstone. Clementine (13), staying on as the new schoolmarm, says goodbye to Wyatt as he rides away.

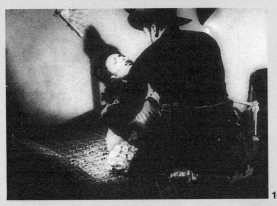

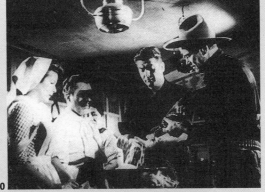

9

10

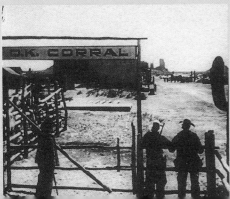

11

12

13

The Third Man

Directed by Carol Reed, 1949
Prod co: (Alexander Korda, David O. Selznick for) London Films. **prod:** Carol Reed. **assoc prod:** Hugh Perceval. **sc:** Graham Greene. **photo:** Robert Krasker. **add photo:** John Wilcox, Stan Pavey. **ed:** Oswald Hafenrichter. **art dir:** Vincent Korda, Joseph Bato, John Hawkesworth. **mus:** Anton Karas. **sd:** John Cox. **ass dir:** Guy Hamilton. **r/t:** 104 mins.
Cast: Joseph Cotten (*Holly Martins*), Orson Welles (*Harry Lime*), Alida Valli (*Anna Schmidt*), Trevor Howard (*Major Calloway*), Paul Hoerbiger (*porter*), Ernst Deutsch (*Baron Kurtz*), Erich Ponto (*Dr Winkel*), Wilfred Hyde White (*Crabbit*), Bernard Lee (*Sergeant Paine*), Siegfried Breuer (*Popescu*), Geoffrey Keen (*British policeman*), Annie Rosar (*porter's wife*), Hedwig Bliebtrau (*Anna's 'Old Woman'*), Harbut Helbek (*Hansl*), Alexis Chesnakov (*Brodsky*), Paul Hardtmuth (*hall porter*).

Left: Carol Reed directs the chase scene in the sewers

After they had completed *The Fallen Idol* (1948), director Carol Reed and writer Graham Greene dined with Alexander Korda, who was anxious for them to work on a new film together. Although they agreed on a setting – post-war Vienna – they were stuck for a story until Greene produced an old envelope on which years before he had written a single sentence:

'I had paid my last farewell to Harry a week ago, when his coffin was lowered into the frozen February ground, so it was with incredulity that I saw him pass by, without a sign of recognition, among the host of strangers in the Strand.'

This became the basis of Reed's *The Third Man*, a film that was to take the Grand Prix at the Cannes Film Festival and earn him a third successive British Film Academy Award for Best Picture.

Greene drafted the story as a novel and then, working closely with Reed, turned it into a screenplay. Although it is in many ways a classic Greene tale, with its themes of guilt and disillusionment, corruption and betrayal, Greene himself has been quick to accord to Reed credit for many of the film's memorable qualities. It was Reed who insisted on the bleakly uncompromising ending where Anna, as she leaves Harry's funeral, walks not into Holly's arms in the conventional final clinch, but passed him, staring impassively ahead. It was Reed who discovered the zither-player, Anton Karas, whose 'Harry Lime theme' gave the film a special haunting quality. It was Reed who prevailed on a reluctant Orson Welles to play the comparatively small but pivotal part of Harry Lime. Welles became so enthusiastic about the film that he contributed to the script a much-quoted justification of Harry's criminal activities:

'In Italy for thirty years under the Borgias they had warfare, terror, murder, bloodshed. They produced Michelangelo, Leonardo da Vinci and the Renaissance. In Switzerland they had brotherly love, five hundred years of democracy and peace. And what did that produce – the cuckoo clock. So long, Holly.'

It was, of course, also Carol Reed who gave remarkable visual life to Greene's brilliantly wrought script, a perfect marriage of word and image, sound and symbol. Holly's odyssey in search of a truth that is to destroy his oldest friend, the girl they both love and, in a sense, Holly himself, is conducted against the background of post-war Vienna, unforgettably evoked by Robert Krasker's powerful chiaroscuro photography which won him a deserved Oscar. The vast, echoing, empty baroque buildings that serve as military headquarters and decaying lodging houses are a melancholy reminder of the Old Vienna, the city of Strauss waltzes and Hapsburg elegance, plunged, in the aftermath of war, into a nightmare world of political intrigue, racketeering and murder. The shadowed, narrow streets and the jagged bomb-sites are the haunt of black marketeers, vividly portrayed inhabitants of a dislocated society. There is a powerful symbolism, too, in the places where Harry makes his appearances: a giant ferris wheel from which he looks down contemptuously at the scuttling mortals, and the Viennese sewers where, after a breathtaking and sharply edited final chase, he is cornered, rat-like, and dispatched.

The angled shooting, atmospheric locations, and sombre shadow-play eloquently convey the pervading aura of tension, mystery and corruption. It is an aura enhanced rather than dissipated by flashes of black humour, such as the sequence in which Holly, bustled by strangers into a car and believing himself kidnapped, discovers he is being taken to address a cultural gathering, the members of which think he is a famous novelist.

The cast is superlative, with the four stars outstanding: Joseph Cotten as decent, dogged, simple, faithful Holly; Alida Valli as the wonderfully enigmatic Anna; Trevor Howard as the shrewd, determined, quietly spoken military policeman Calloway; and Orson Welles as the fascinating Harry Lime. *The Third Man* was one of the peaks of post-war British film-making and remains a flawlessly crafted, timelessly perfect work of art.
JEFFREY RICHARDS

1

2

Holly Martins, a writer of hack Westerns, arrives in Vienna to look for his friend Harry Lime, only to be told that Harry has been killed in a street accident. Holly attends the funeral (1) and is questioned by military policeman Major Calloway (2), who tells him that Harry was a racketeer selling penicillin so diluted that it caused the deaths of sick children.

Holly sets out to find the truth and visits Harry's girlfriend, actress Anna Schmidt (3), who suggests that Harry's death may not have been accidental. An elderly porter reports seeing a mysterious third man at the scene of the accident (4); next day the porter is found dead. Holly is chased by two thugs but escapes. Leaving Anna's apartment, he sees Harry in the shadows (5) and realizes he is 'the third man'. Harry's coffin is exhumed and found to contain the body of a police informer.

Harry arranges to meet Holly and offers to buy his silence (6). But when Calloway arrests Anna (7) (who has a forged passport) and plans to deport her behind the Iron Curtain, Holly, who is in love with her, betrays Harry to the police in return for her release. A chase through the sewers underneath the city (8), ends with Holly shooting Harry dead. Anna attends the funeral and then walks away past Holly without speaking to him (9).

3

4

5

6

7

8

9

Few films make effective reading when their words are divorced from their images. And if one is found that does, the tendency is immediately to assume that there must be something wrong with it. Certainly *Kind Hearts and Coronets* has often posed this kind of a problem: it allows such weight to the spoken word that it has often been thought of as literary and uncinematic. And yet, at this distance of time from its first appearance in 1949, it stands out as the least faded, most indubitably alive of all the British films of its era. And, perhaps because cinema criticism is now a lot less hidebound by simplistic theories of what is or is not 'cinematic' than it once was, it would probably not occur to anyone seeing the film for the first time to query its 'summit meeting' of words and images or worry about how it could somehow be made to fit into a world-view shaped by neo-realism.

The corollary of this is that today's audience would not realize how exceptional the film was in its time; but part of Robert Hamer's stated principle in making it was that it should be 'a film not noticeably similar to any previously made in the English language'. Hamer had

been a film editor, then a writer, then – as one of Michael Balcon's bright young men at Ealing – a director, making his debut with an episode in the composite picture *Dead of Night* (1945). He had followed it with a couple of solo features, *Pink String and Sealing Wax* (1945), a period murder story, and *It Always Rains on Sunday* (1947), a downbeat study of working-class life which he also wrote; the elegance of the first and the social perceptiveness of the second retrospectively provide a hint of what was to come. No-one, however, could have guessed what Hamer was up to when he discovered and began to adapt the little-known Edwardian novel, *Israel Rank* – a rather self-consciously decadent piece written by Roy Horniman (a follower of Oscar Wilde) – having decided that it had the makings of a film comedy.

In adapting it Hamer remained true to the period of the story and to the allegiance to Wilde. Otherwise, only the basic plot of the novel was retained: the plight of a young man whose mother has married beneath her and been cast out by her family, and his determination to get revenge and repair his spoilt fortunes by murdering his way through a

Kind Hearts

When the younger daughter of the Duke of Chalfont runs off with a penniless Italian singer her family disowns her. She tells her son Louis about his grand forbears but, denied any aid from her family, he has to work in a draper's shop. Stung by the family's refusal to recognize kinship with his mother – even when she dies – he determines to get his own back and to impress his suburban girlfriend Sibella (1) by disposing of all who stand between him and the family title.

First, he murders his most obnoxious cousin (2) during a dirty weekend at Henley, and then blows up another cousin, an amateur photographer (3). A cleric uncle is poisoned (4); a suffragette aunt it shot down in her balloon (5); a soldier uncle is booby-trapped while recounting his most famous campaign (6); and a sailor uncle goes down

1

2

3

4

7

8

9

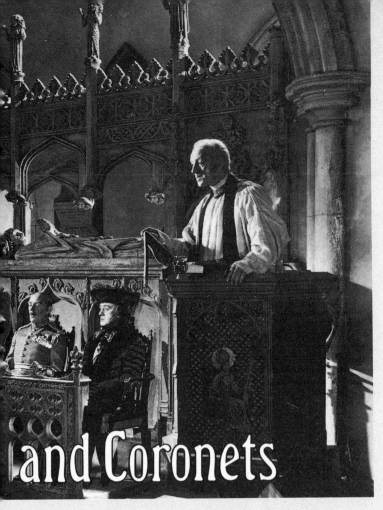

and Coronets

Directed by Robert Hamer, 1949
Prod co: Ealing. **prod:** Michael Balcon. **assoc prod:** Michael Relph. **sc:** Robert Hamer, John Dighton, from the novel *Israel Rank* by Roy Horniman. **photo:** Douglas Slocombe, Jeff Seaholme. **sp eff:** Sydney Pearson, Geoffrey Dickinson. **ed:** Peter Tanner. **art dir:** William Kellner. **mus:** Ernest Irving, extract from Mozart's *Don Giovanni* played by The Philharmonic Orchestra, conducted by Ernest Irving. **cost:** Anthony Mendleson. **sd:** Stephen Dalby, John Mitchell. **ass dir:** Norman Priggen. **r/t:** 106 minutes.
Cast: Dennis Price (*Louis Mazzini*), Valerie Hobson (*Edith d'Ascoyne*), Joan Greenwood (*Sibella*), Alec Guinness (*Ethelred, Duke of Chalfont; Lord Ascoyne d'Ascoyne; The Reverend Lord Henry d'Ascoyne; General Lord Rufus d'Ascoyne; Admiral Lord Horatio d'Ascoyne; Ascoyne d'Ascoyne; Henry d'Ascoyne; Lady Agatha d'Ascoyne*), Audrey Fildes (*Mama*), Miles Malleson (*hangman*), Clive Morton (*prison governor*), John Penrose (*Lionel*), Cecil Ramage (*Crown Counsel*), Hugh Griffith (*Lord High Steward*), John Salew (*Mr Perkins*), Eric Messiter (*Burgoyne*), Lyn Evans (*farmer*), Barbara Leake (*schoolmistress*), Peggy Ann Clifford (*Maud*), Anne Valery (*girl in the punt*), Arthur Lowe (*reporter*).

with his ship after a collision at sea (7). This makes Louis heir apparent to the Chalfont title, and the accepted fiancé of Edith (the photographer cousin's widow).

Just as Louis is achieving his goal by shooting the present duke (8) – whereupon the last remaining uncle expires on hearing he has succeeded to the dukedom – Sibella's husband dies in suspicious circumstances and he is charged with the one

Above: two down, six to go – the funeral service for the second d'Ascoyne cousin

murder he didn't do. Sibella agrees to get him acquitted if he will dispose of Edith and make her the next duchess (9). All goes according to plan, but there is still the problem of Louis' compromising memoirs (10) which he has absent-mindedly left in his prison cell on being freed (11) . . .

whole family of unspeakable relatives on his way to a dukedom. In the novel this involves a lot of Nietzschean attitudinizing on the part of the self-styled superman hero; in the film it is all distilled into an exquisitely subversive comedy of manners, decorated with a constant sparkle of verbal wit such as Wilde himself would not have disowned.

But that is not all. The film's visual wit perfectly complements the verbal. If the tone is established primarily by the dialogue and by the ruthless Louis' voice-over commentary on the action, it is still true that the best effects are produced by a knowing counterpoint of word and image. A typical example of this is when Louis' tea-time conversation with his cousin's chilly wife (soon to be his) is accompanied by the gradual appearance of a column of smoke indicating that something nasty has happened to his cousin in the woodshed. Elsewhere Hamer's precise selection of what details to show us in the behaviour of his characters lets the audience know just how to read every move in this cool but by no means unemotional game.

The performances are, of course,

superb Dennis Price as the dandyish, but under it all slightly demonic, Louis was never better, and neither were Joan Greenwood and Valerie Hobson, perfectly cast as the two contrasting women in his life. Alec Guinness' extraordinary feat, playing eight members of the d'Ascoyne family, has been much remarked on, but the most remarkable thing about it is that it is virtually unnoticeable. So exactly is each member of the family portrayed that, while seeing the film, the spectator is aware only of the diversity and believability, not of the one actor who achieves it. But, first and foremost, the film is the personal creation of Robert Hamer, as close to a genuine *auteur* film as the British cinema has ever come.

Though some of Hamer's later films were enjoyable – notably *Father Brown* (1954), which reunited him with Guinness and Greenwood – he never had another comparable chance to express his elegant, uncomfortable wit in the context of a generally conservative British cinema. A pity – but at least *Kind Hearts and Coronets* remains a masterpiece, and unique.

JOHN RUSSELL TAYLOR

5

6

10

11

HIS ONLY FRIEND WAS HIS GUN...

HIS ONLY REFUGE — A WOMAN'S HEART!

GREGORY PECK in THE GUNFIGHTER

Helen WESTCOTT · Millard MITCHELL · Jean PARKER · HENRY KING · NUNNALLY JOHNSON

KARL MALDEN·SKIP HOMEIER·ANTHONY ROSS·VERNA FELTON·ELLEN CORBY·RICHARD JAECKEL · WILLIAM BOWERS & WILLIAM SELLERS · William Bowers · Andre De Toth

CENTURY

Directed by Henry King, 1950
Prod co: 20th Century-Fox. **prod:** Nunnally Johnson. **sc:** William Bowers, William Sellers, from a story by William Bowers and Andre De Toth. **photo:** Arthur Miller. **ed:** Barbara McLean. **art dir:** Lyle R. Wheeler, Richard Irvine. **mus:** Alfred Newman. **r/t:** 84 minutes.
Cast: Gregory Peck (*Jimmy Ringo*), Helen Westcott (*Peggy Walsh*), Millard Mitchell (*Marshall Mark Strett*), Jean Parker (*Molly*), Mae Marsh (*Mrs O'Brien*), Karl Malden (*Mac*), Skip Homeier (*Hunt Bromley*), Anthony Ross (*Charlie*), Verna Felton (*Mrs Pennyfeather*), Ellen Corby (*Mrs Devlin*), Richard Jaeckel (*Eddie*), Alan Hale Jr (*first brother*), David Clarke (*second brother*), John Pickard (*third brother*), D.G. Norman (*Jimmy*), Angela Clarke (*Mac's wife*), Cliff Clark (*Jerry Marlowe*), Jean Inness (*Alice Marlowe*), Eddie Ehrhart (*Archie*), Albert Morin (*Pablo*).

Like the celebrated but not necessarily more memorable Westerns that came immediately after it – *High Noon* (1952), *Shane* (1953), *Rio Bravo* (1959) – *The Gunfighter* was a highly self-conscious film. It quite knowingly took up and restated themes that had been present in this genre almost from the beginning and subtly indicated, here and there, that its makers knew that they were doing so. As a result, a film that might have been dismissed as a cliché became a work that the knowledgeable public – and reviewers – could embrace for its classicism without spoiling the groundlings' fun.

The theme is that old favourite, the reluctant gunman – a man fecklessly trying to outrun his unwanted reputation as a fast hand with a six-shooter. He discovers, in the course of the film, that even his home town, where his estranged wife is raising his son not to know who his father is, will not offer him protection from his past. He carries with him the Western loner's most basic dream of the little ranch far, far away where he can settle down at last, as well as the loner's hope that he can pass through streets and bar-rooms unrecognized by the kids and punks who want to make their reputations by beating him to the draw.

In short, the film covers familiar country. Why, then, does *The Gunfighter* linger so pleasingly in the memory? One reason is its excellent dialogue. When Eddie threatens the weary Jimmy Ringo, the latter's contempt is crisply stated: 'Why don't you button up your breeches,' he advises the youth, 'and go home.' Later, when he is discussing the discrepancy between his fame and his fortune, he sadly reflects: 'Here I am, 35, and I ain't even got a good watch.' There is a homeliness in his speech, as befits his time and place, but a certain freshness and unexpectedness in it, too. Throughout the film Gregory Peck is laconic without lapsing into inarticulateness and, for once, he gets to make his point without having to make a speech. He responds almost gratefully to this opportunity to play integrity without having to talk about it endlessly.

Indeed the decency of that Lincolnesque image of his, which he cannot help but drag with him from film to film, provides a curious subtext against which to play a character who is, at bottom, a murderer for hire. Peck plays this contrast without overplaying it. The austere, not to say stark, *mise-en-scène* derives from the veteran director Henry King, for whom Peck created his other memorable performance, that of the American officer breaking under the strain of sending his fliers

to certain death in the bombing raids of *Twelve O'Clock High* (1949). King has often seemed a director better than his assignments, but in *The Gunfighter* he had a project that perfectly matched his essential modesty and directness of understatement. There is a tightness and a tension to this small, black-and-white film that is admirably and efficiently developed without mannerism and, in particular contrast to *Shane* without self-importance.

There is, of course, a sub-theme to the film: one of particular relevance in the United States in 1950. It had to do with betrayal. The Peck character, though he had surely done some bad things, was not a bad man. As much as anything, he was undone by a shift in the values of respectable society. In other words, he had been honoured for his deadly skill at his deadly trade when nice people had need of him to fight their battles for them. Now that they no longer require his services they will not come to his aid as he seeks peace from continued professional challenges. In the end he

dies precisely because his friends and neighbours turn him out and place him back on the road that can only lead to oblivion. Perhaps this was a metaphorical expression of contempt for the way that Hollywood in particular, and American society in general, was, at the moment of the film's release, turning against prominent leftists who, only a few years before, had seemed to be speaking for generally held liberal values and now found themselves alone and deserted by people who had once stood behind them. It is, of course, one of the values of *The Gunfighter* that it does not insist on this point – thus contrasting with *High Noon*'s heavy-handed harping on a similar parallel – and can be enjoyed simply as a well-made, highly professional genre exercise.

RICHARD SCHICKEL

Below: the director Henry King prepares the reunion scene, where Jimmy Ringo finally gets to see his wife, with Gregory Peck and Helen Westcott

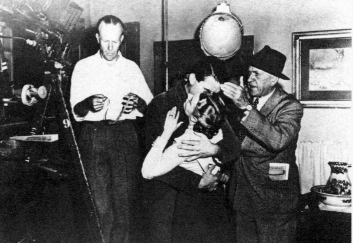

1

2

3

4

Jimmy Ringo, a well-known gunfighter, walks into a bar where Eddie, a young hot-head trying to impress his friends, challenges him to a draw (1). Ringo is forced to kill him. He leaves town, meets Eddie's three brothers who are seeking revenge, disarms them and rides on.

He arrives in Cayenne where he meets Mark Strett, a former member of his gang, now the town marshal. Strett asks him to leave town, but Ringo says that he has come to see his wife Peggy and son Jimmy whom he has not seen for eight years. No-one except Strett and an old friend, Molly, knows that Peggy is Ringo's wife and Peggy has not even told her son that Ringo is his father.

While Strett goes to ask Peggy whether she will see Ringo, word gets around that a famous gunfighter is in town. Outside the saloon where Ringo is waiting, people gather – only to be shoo'd away periodically by the anxious bartender (2). Strett's mission is unsuccessful so Ringo asks Molly to intercede on his behalf (3).

While he waits for an answer, he is taunted by the town punk, Hunt Bromley (4), but Ringo frightens him off. Molly brings Peggy to meet Ringo (5); he begs her to come back to him, promising to keep out of trouble for a year and then send for her. He also sees his son again (6).

Meanwhile Eddie's brothers arrive in town (7). But just as they are about to shoot Ringo the marshal's deputy arrest them. As Ringo mounts his horse to leave town, Bromley catches him at a disadvantage and shoots him (8). Before he dies, Ringo asks Strett not to arrest Bromley but rather to leave him to the miseries of the life of a gunfighter (9).

5

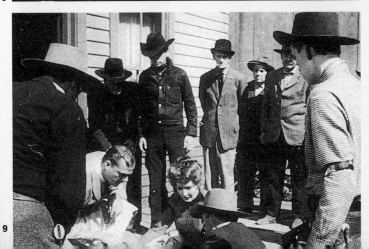

6

8

9

STANLEY KRAMER PRODUCTIONS presents

GARY COOPER

THERE IS NOTHING UNDER THE SUN
LIKE THE HIGH ADVENTURE OF "HIGH NOON"!

"HIGH NOON"

STANLEY KRAMER PRODUCTIONS presents GARY COOPER in "HIGH NOON" with THOMAS MITCHELL · LLOYD BRIDGES · KATY JURADO · GRACE KELLY · OTTO KRUGER Lon Chaney · Henry Morgan · DIRECTED BY FRED ZINNEMANN · Screen Play by Carl Foreman · Music Composed and Directed by Dimitri Tiomkin · Director of Photography Floyd Crosby, A.S.C. · RELEASED THRU UNITED ARTISTS

HIGH NOON

Around 1950–51 the screenwriter Carl Foreman composed a scenario about an ageing marshal abandoned by his townsfolk and his bride and forced to stand alone against a team of gunmen. The rights of *The Tin Star*, a similar story by John W. Cunningham, were bought to avoid copyright litigation and production began on *High Noon* – a modest, low-budget, black-and-white Western that was to be the last of several collaborations between Foreman and independent producer Stanley Kramer. The director Fred Zinnemann, who had worked with them on *The Men* (1950), was signed and Gary Cooper – at 51 a fading star – was cast as Will Kane, the hero.

It was the McCarthy era and Foreman, an alleged communist, had already clashed with the House Un-American Activities Committee. During the filming of *High Noon* he was subpoenaed but refused to name names or comment on his political persuasions – an action that reputedly won him the admiration of Gary Cooper, even though Cooper was a noted anti-communist and friendly witness. Foreman was eventually blacklisted, snubbed by Hollywood and obliged to continue his film career in Europe. It has since been fashionable to emphasize the fact that *High Noon* is a bitter allegory of McCarthyism, with Kane as the hunted man who obeys his conscience and the cowardly people of Hadleyville as the American public that turned a blind eye to the witch-hunts. At the end of the film Kane, having dispatched his assailants, drops his marshal's badge into the dust – supposedly Foreman's way of showing how highly he regarded American justice and society.

Despite this, however, the action on the screen allows no time for the audience to worry about allegorical content. *High Noon* is confined to 85 minutes in the life of the small town, beginning around 10.35 on the morning of Kane's wedding and proceeding to just after 12.00. It consists of Kane's agonizing wait for his pursuers to arrive on the noon train, the intolerably tense and protracted gunfight in which every blind corner and alleyway promises a bullet in the stomach for the lone marshal, and the brief ending when he holds his wife in his arms and turns his back on the town. The accent on time running out for Kane is clearly stated by frequent close-ups of ticking clocks that bring noon tantalizingly nearer and give vocal and visual expression to the torturous heart-beat pulse of the story.

The ticking stabs at Kane, brilliantly played by Cooper. There is no mistaking how afraid the marshal is: his walk down the sun-beaten streets becomes increasingly mannered and stiff as time leaks away, but it acquires a strange and impressive resoluteness that stems less from ignorant courage than from a refusal to give in to the sickening fear within. At one point he goes into his office and buries **9**

his head in his hands, sobbing. However this momentary capitulation is only an admission of mortality. It is a suggestion of weakness that merely emphasizes how resilient the man is, for soon afterwards he destroys his enemies – even if his wife has to lend a hand.

Similarly in *Shane* (1953), the hero buys a soda-pop in front of jeering cowboys in the store, displaying a misleading humility against which to contrast the deadly ability of his fists and gun. Both Kane and Shane were central figures in the new adult Western of the Fifties, their colossal reserves of courage and strength being occasionally at odds with characteristics like fear, pacifism and gentleness.

Kane must – and does – overcome not only his friendlessness and fear of death, but also the mortifying desertion by Amy, his bride of a few minutes. After the preview of *High Noon* met with a disappointing response, Kramer asked the composer Dmitri Tiomkin to write a song for the film. He came up with 'Do Not Forsake Me, Oh My Darlin'', an aching ballad which was added to the soundtrack to bridge various scenes. With its throbbing tune and recurring line of desperation – 'What will I do if you leave me?' – as if addressed by Kane to Amy, it provides a chilling motif, ebbing away at moments of despair to suggest the real reason for the torment etched on Kane's face.

In reality Gary Cooper had an ulcer at the time and was in considerable pain throughout filming. In contributing to Kane's tightlipped wretchedness it also helped Cooper to a second Oscar and revived his career as a Western star. The film also won Oscars for Best Song, Best Score and Best Editing and was a massive box-office success.

Political allegory, suspenseful psychological Western or apotheosis of nervous heroism, *High Noon* is, by any standards, a work of enduring excellence and its depiction of Will Kane patrolling the Hadleyville main street is one of the most memorable images from American cinema.

GRAHAM FULLER

Directed by Fred Zinnemann, 1952
Prod: Stanley Kramer. **sc:** Carl Foreman, loosely based on the story *The Tin Star* by John W. Cunningham. **photo:** Floyd Crosby. **ed:** Elmo Williams. **ass ed:** Harry Gerstad. **art dir:** Rudolph Sternad. **mus:** Dmitri Tiomkin. **song:** 'Do Not Forsake Me Oh My Darlin'' by Dmitri Tiomkin, Ned Washington, sung by Tex Ritter. **sd:** Jean Speak. **ass dir:** Emmett Emerson. **r/t** 85 minutes.
Cast: Gary Cooper (*Will Kane*), Thomas Mitchell (*Jonas Henderson*), Lloyd Bridges (*Harvey Pell*), Katy Jurado (*Helen Ramirez*), Grace Kelly (*Amy Kane*), Otto Kruger (*Percy Mettrick*), Lon Chaney (*Martin Howe*), Henry Morgan (*William Fuller*), Ian Macdonald (*Frank Miller*), Eve McVeagh (*Mildred Fuller*), Harry Shannon (*Cooper*), Lee Van Cleef (*Jack Colby*), Bob Wilke (*James Pierce*), Sheb Woolley (*Ben Miller*), Tom London (*Sam*), Ted Stanhope (*station master*), Larry Blake (*Gillis*), William Phillips (*barber*), Jeanne Blackford (*Mrs Henderson*), James Milligan (*baker*), Cliff Clark (*weaver*), Ralph Reed (*Johnny*), William Newell (*drunk*), Lucien Prival (*bartender*), Guy Beach (*Fred*), Howland Chamberlin (*hotel clerk*), Morgan Farley (*minister*), Virginia Christine (*Mrs Simpson*), Virginia Farmer (*Mrs Fletcher*), Jack Elam (*Charlie*), Paul Dubov (*Scott*), Harry Harvey (*Coy*), Tim Graham (*Sawyer*), Nolan Leary (*Lewis*), Tom Greenway (*Ezra*), Dick Elliott (*Kibbee*), John Doucette (*Trumbull*).

2

3

5

7

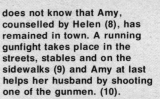

8

At 10.35 on a hot June morning in 1865 Will Kane, marshal of Hadleyville, marries a Mormon girl Amy (1). News immediately arrives that Frank Miller – an outlaw convicted by Kane five years earlier – has been pardoned, released from jail and is returning to seek revenge (2).

Although Kane has announced his retirement and is under no obligation to stay, he decides that it is his duty to protect the town from Miller and his three gunmen who are already waiting for their leader up at the station. However, Amy's religion has taught her to deplore violence and she tells Kane she is leaving on the noon train.

Going to the saloon and church to drum up support Kane finds that no-one is prepared to join forces with him (3). Everyone has an excuse for not fighting Miller, including the mayor and Kane's jealous deputy Harvey – beaten in a fight with the marshal when he tries to prevent Kane making a lone stand (4). Helen, Harvey's girl and a former lover of both Kane and Miller, vents her disgusted anger on the deputy (5) and decides to leave him and Hadleyville.

At noon the train brings Miller to Hadleyville (6). Kane – bruised, frightened and alone – prepares to take on the four men (7). He does not know that Amy, counselled by Helen (8), has remained in town. A running gunfight takes place in the streets, stables and on the sidewalks (9) and Amy at last helps her husband by shooting one of the gunmen. (10).

Kane manages to kill the other three. Embracing Amy (11) he flings his badge in the dust (12) and the couple ride away on a buckboard.

10

11

12

COLUMBIA PICTURES presents

MARLON BRANDO
On The Waterfront
AN ELIA KAZAN PRODUCTION

KARL MALDEN · LEE J. COBB with **ROD STEIGER · PAT HENNING** introducing **EVA MARIE SAINT**
Produced by **SAM SPIEGEL** Screen Play by **BUDD SCHULBERG** Music by **LEONARD BERNSTEIN** Directed by **ELIA KAZAN**

Directed by Elia Kazan, 1954
Prod co: Horizon. **prod:** Sam Spiegel. **sc:** Budd Schulberg, from articles by Malcolm Johnson. **photo:** Boris Kaufman. **ed:** Arthur E. Milford. **art dir:** Richard Day. **mus:** Leonard Bernstein. **r/t:** 107 minutes.
Cast: Marlon Brando (*Terry Malloy*), Eva Marie Saint (*Edie Doyle*), Karl Malden (*Father Barry*), Lee J. Cobb (*Johnny Friendly*), Rod Steiger (*Charley Malloy*), Pat Henning (*'Kayo' Dugan*), Leif Erikson (*Glover*), James Westerfield (*Big Mac*), John Heldabrand (*Mutt*), Rudy Bond (*Moose*), John Hamilton (*'Pop' Doyle*).

If *On the Waterfront* presents fewer problems for critics today than it did when it was first released, it can only be because the subsequent careers of many of its principals have clarified their original intentions. The film itself remains ambiguous. With its seedy dockland setting it threw down the gauntlet to the European neo-realist cinema and its apparent involvement with the sometimes uncomfortable realities of working-class life echoed the political and sociological pretensions of neo-realism. The American critic Pauline Kael wrote that *On the Waterfront* 'came as a public shock because Hollywood films had stayed away from the real America' – as if to say that the mere presentation of events loosely based on contemporary labour history was enough to guarantee a realism absent from films about cowboys, cops or rich people.

Of course, dockland life was not generally considered glamorous and trade unionism was a subject not often mentioned in Hollywood films. In these respects *On the Waterfront* was something of a breakthrough. Yet the realism, which Kael observed back in 1955 was little more than a superficial gloss resulting from location shooting, low-key lighting and the use of a number of generally unknown actors. The film's concern for contemporary political issues was evidenced by a pompous introduction extolling the living strength of American democracy. In context this seems like blatant political propaganda. Elia Kazan, the film's director, was a very friendly witness at the 1952 Hollywood Un-American Activities Committee. Reversing an earlier, principled decision, he admitted having been a member of the Communist Party in the Thirties and proceeded to name many of his former colleagues as one-time Party members. His career in Hollywood went from strength to strength in the years following 1952.

It may not be too fanciful to see in *On the Waterfront* a thinly veiled allegory of Kazan's new-found anti-communism. The dockers become the Hollywood community, the gang become the Communist Party and Terry Malloy, the hero, is Kazan himself. Yet there is no irony in the handling of the plot. Either way, the parallel offers another argument against *On the Waterfront*'s much vaunted realism. Budd Schulberg, the writer, may have fashioned his story out of news-feature material provided by the journalist Malcolm Johnson but, as even *Time* magazine pointed out when *On the Waterfront* was released, he and Kazan had chipped away at this

material until a fairy story emerged. Real racketeering and the struggle against it were never like this. Political realities were not allowed to undermine the simplistic moral struggle between good and evil. The film is laden with straightforward Christian symbolism and carries the metaphor of Terry's caged pigeons with some signs of weariness. The one genuine originality of *On the Waterfront* remains in its choice of setting and Boris Kaufman's evocative cinematography – otherwise it might just as easily be a clichéd Western (complete with civilized schoolma'am in the shape of Eva Marie Saint) or, for that matter, a crass apologia for Kazan's actions in the face of the McCarthyite witch-hunt.

It was Brando's sixth film and the first to win an Academy Award for him. If today the performance seems less convincing and more mannered than it did at the time of the film's first release, it must be remembered that *On the Waterfront* was the peak of Brando's meteoric early film career. Terry Malloy was an amalgam of Stanley Kowalski from *A Streetcar Named Desire* (1951), Emiliano Zapata from *Viva Zapata!* (1952) and Johnny from *The Wild One* (1953). As one critic put it at the time, Brando (which is to say Terry Malloy) was by turns 'thuggish, vulnerable, gentle and vicious.' He was also crusader and coward, traitor and betrayed – in fact, the perfect existentialist hero of the time. It is difficult to imagine anybody but Brando carrying off the classic scene in the back of a cab when Terry Malloy discovers the extent of his brother's perfidy. 'Oh Charley, Oh Charley,' he says, 'you don't understand. I could have had class. I could have been a con-

tender. I could have been somebody, instead of a bum, which is what I am.'

Brando's Terry Malloy may be quirky but it is a virtuoso performance. It comes as something of a surprise to find that the film's producer, Sam Spiegel, originally wanted Frank Sinatra (hot from his success as Private Maggio in *From Here to Eternity*, 1953) to play the role.

But then, if establishment Hollywood had had its way, *On the Waterfront* would have been shot in California. That alone should be borne in mind when it comes to assessing the significance of the Academy Award-winning picture for 1954.   GARY HERMAN

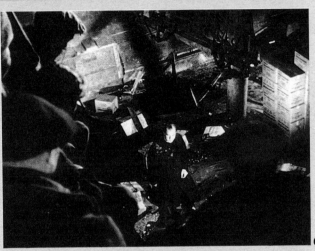

Ex-boxer Terry Malloy lives and works on New York's dockside. His one uncomplicated pleasure in life is derived from the pigeons he keeps on the roof of his tenement block. Terry's brother Charley, 'The Gent', is the senior lieutenant of the gangsters who control the Longshoreman's Union. At Charley's instigation, Terry (1) lures Joey Doyle, a dock-worker who will not accept gang control of the union, to his death. As a result, Terry has a secure relationship with the gang-leader Johnny Friendly (2).

Although everyone suspects that the gang killed Joey, no-one will talk; but Joey's sister Edie, just home from college, and the local priest, Father Barry, are determined to find the truth and convict Joey's murderers

Terry meets Edie and finds himself attracted to her. Spying for the gang, he attends a meeting called by Father Barry and Edie to begin a campaign against the gang (3). Edie does not know about Terry's part in her brother's death and asks him to help find the murderers and bring them to justice (4).

The one person prepared to testify against the gang is killed in an 'accident' at the docks and Father Barry appeals for more help (5).

Terry is increasingly drawn towards betrayal and he tells Edie

about his involvement in Joey's death (6).

Charley is delegated by the gang to prevent Terry betraying them, but Terry shames Charley into letting him go by reminding him of how he ruined Terry's boxing career. Having failed to guarantee his brother's loyalty, Charley is murdered (7) and Terry agrees to testify at the hearing against the gang (8).

The morning after his appearance before the Crime Commission, Terry arrives at the dock to find himself confronted by the gang. He is badly beaten-up (9). However, he emerges bloody, but unbowed (10), to lead the dockers into work.

29

LES 7 SAMOURAÏ

Un film d'AKIRO KUROSAWA

seemed innovatory to Western audiences especially when compared with other Japanese films, where the images seemed to be highly stylized, adopting a pictorial formalism derived from Japanese painting. Attempting to seize action on the wing, uncertain in advance which of his cameras would actually capture it, Kurosawa naturally could not compose for the frame with the precision and care expended upon every image by Ozu or Mizoguchi. But to conclude from this that Kurosawa is un-Japanese is false. The formalism of much Japanese art is based on suspended movement: freeze any frame of *Seven Samurai*, and you have the makings of a Hokusai woodcut.

Similarly, although the film seems as clear as any standard Western, it enshrines a number of subtle ambiguities. When the village emissaries first see Kambei, for instance, they watch in amazement as, prior to posing as a priest to trap the homicidal thief, he has his head shaved. In Japanese custom, this means that a samurai is either disgraced, or about to leave the world to become a priest. Building on this enigma, since Kambei is clearly bent on following neither course, Kurosawa proceeds to show how he is in fact following both. As a samurai, in

Directed by Akira Kurosawa, 1954
Prod co: Toho. **prod:** Shojiro Motoki. **sc:** Shinobu Hashimoto, Hideo Oguni, Akira Kurosawa. **photo:** Asakazu Nakai. **art dir:** So Matsuyama. **fencing dir:** Yoshio Sugino. **archery dir:** Tenori Kaneko, Shigeru Endo. **mus:** Fumio Hayasaka. **sd:** Fumio Yanoguchi. **r/t:** 160 minutes. Japanese title: *Shichinin No Samurai.* Released in GB/USA as *Seven Samurai.*
Cast: Takashi Shimura (*Kambei*), Toshiro Mifune (*Kikuchiyo*), Yoshio Inaba (*Gorobei*), Seiji Miyaguchi (*Kyuzo*), Minoru Chiaki (*Heihachi*), Daisuke Kato (*Shichiroji*), Ko Kimura (*Katsushiro*), Kamatari Fujiwara (*Manzo*), Kuninori Kodo (*Gisaku*), Bokuzen Hidari (*Yohei*), Yoshio Kosugi (*Mosuke*), Yoshio Tsuchiya (*Rikichi*), Keiji Sakakida (*Gosaku*), Keiko Tsushima (*Shino*), Toranosuke Ogawa (*grandfather*), Yu Akitsu (*husband*), Noriko Sengoku (*wife*), Gen Shimizu (*masterless samurai*), Jun Tatari (*coolie*), Atsushi Watanabe (*vendor*), Sojin Kamiyama (*minstrel*), Kichijiro Ueda, Shimpei Takagi, Akira Tani (*bandits*).

Akira Kurosawa has always been the most problematic of the major Japanese directors. Having made the first real breakthrough for Japanese cinema in the West with *Rashomon* (1950), he continued to enjoy a commercial success that was (and still is) denied to Kenji Mizoguchi and Yasujiro Ozu. There were ample reasons for this, not least the clear accessibility of Kurosawa's work, (where the influence of John Ford's Westerns is unmistakable), the source material which is often familiar (Shakespeare, Dostoyevsky, Gorky), and the distinctly cosmopolitan sensibility of his films.

The problem was highlighted when *Shichinin No Samurai* (*Seven Samurai*) became a worldwide hit in 1954. Although Kurosawa cannot be said to have been critically misjudged, the lingering suspicion that he was indulging in un-Japanese activities in order to court Western favour seemed to be confirmed by the ease with which *Seven Samurai* took to being remade as a Hollywood Western, *The Magnificent Seven* (1960). There was also the question of the techniques used in the film.

Claiming with some justification that Mizoguchi's historical epics were magnificent *except* for their

battle scenes (usually either elided or dismissed in a handful of tableaux) Kurosawa planned to redress the balance in filming the carnage and confusion of the battles in *Seven Samurai*. To give the audience the feeling that they were present in the past, watching something that was actually happening rather than represented, he therefore pioneered the use of multiple cameras (filming scenes from several angles so as to be able to select the most vivid take of any given moment), and of the telephoto lens (giving the illusion that the action is much closer to camera than it actually is).

He also made systematic use of jump-cuts in editing to speed up the action (a character is asked a question in one location; his reply comes in another, with a different scene already under way) six years before Jean-Luc Godard 'revolutionized' cinema by doing the same thing in *A Bout de Souffle* (1960, *Breathless*). The result is a film in perpetual motion, moving to and fro with such concentrated intensity that the threat of violence remains inescapably present until it explodes in the final sequence.

All these techniques are, of course, commonplace now, especially on television. At the time, they

3

7

effect a hired killer in the lawless society of the times, Kambei *is* disgraced already; and through the wisdom and charity he displays on behalf of the villagers, he *becomes* in effect a priest.

In one of the nicest ironies of the film (teaching a social lesson which *The Magnificent Seven* omits entirely), it is the halfwit Kikuchiyo, the 'innocent', who reveals this truth to Kambei. When the seven samurai first arrive, the villagers vanish in terror only to come flocking back for protection when a bandit attack is threatened. Just as the outraged Kikuchiyo succeeds in shaming the villagers for their illogicality, the samurai take umbrage after discovering a hidden store of weapons indicating that the villagers have been killing and robbing wandering samurai.

'One who has never been hunted wouldn't understand,' says Kambei, explaining the viewpoint of the unhappy, unemployed samurai, wandering and weary, an easy prey to the very people they had once kept firmly in order.

'Do you think farmers are angels?' the angry Kikuchiyo replies, ending his long, impassioned tirade with irrefutable logic:

'They're mean, stupid and murderous. But then, who made them such beasts? You samurai did it . . .'
TOM MILNE

It is late sixteenth-century Japan. In the troubled times following civil war, the farmers are terrorized by bandits (1) making regular raids on their harvests. Encouraged by their elders the inhabitants of one village (2) at last decide to follow the example of another which reputedly hired samurai to fight for them.

Watching one samurai deal expertly with a homicidal thief who is holding a child hostage, the emissaries from the village are encouraged by learning that, masterless and hungry, the samurai accepted a payment of two rice balls. Unable to offer money, they nevertheless manage to hire the samurai, Kambei, when he realizes the sacrifices entailed in their proposal to pay three meals a day.

Aided by Katsushiro, an admiring young disciple, Kambei recruits individually (3) four more unattached samurai – Shichiroji, Gorobei, Heihachi and Kyuzo – who accept the terms out of a mixture of pride, hunger and respect for Kambei. Followed by Kikuchiyo, a half-crazy braggart who refuses to take no for an answer (4), the six are escorted to the village. There Kikuchiyo, himself a farmer's son, is instrumental in establishing a mutual trust between the villagers and the samurai they have learned to fear.

Defences are prepared, the villagers are trained. Katsushiro, meanwhile, has struck up a friendship with one of the village girls (5). When three bandit scouts are killed (6) before they can tell the bandits about the new defences, their horses are used by Gorobei, Kyuzo and Kikuchiyo in a successful raid on the bandit hideout, though Gorobei is killed. The bandits finally attack (7) and are wiped out under Kambei's expert leadership in a long and bloody battle (8, 9), in which many villagers are killed. Of the samurai, only Kambei, Shichiroji and Katsushiro survive the bloodshed.

Already forgotten by the farmers, who are back at work in the fields (10), the samurai prepare to leave; but Katsushiro, having fallen in love with a farmer's daughter, decides to remain in the village.

One of the most shocking moments in *Kiss Me Deadly* is when the police detective tells private eye Mike Hammer just what he thinks of him. He tells him that he is a grubby crawler into other people's affairs and underlinen; a man over his head in a situation that is too vast for him to understand. The moment shocks because it reverses the audience's understanding of how it should feel about Hammer.

The average audience would have assumed, however callous and brutal his actions and however sardonically sawn-off his words, that Hammer was somehow on the side of right – as any good private eye in the Chandler tradition ought to be. But Hammer is no Chandler-esque knight in tarnished armour walking erect through mean streets; he was created by Mickey Spillane, a writer with an eye for best-selling sadism. In Hammer is the demeaned perpetuation of the private-investigator ethic.

So articulate is the police detective's distaste that it is obvious that the film's director Robert Aldrich and its screenwriter A. I. Bezzerides feel exactly that way about Hammer too. It is not just that he is an anti-hero, but in his arrogant assumption that his amoral might is right, he is a *fascist* hero. It is as though Aldrich and Bezzerides were using the character in order to repudiate him and all he stands for.

This is just one of the many dazzling brilliances in a movie that was of seminal importance for its time, establishing Aldrich as a cult *auteur* with French critics, and later regarded as a classic *film noir*. On the surface, *Kiss Me Deadly* is a roughneck suspense thriller of enormous ingenuity, but on other levels the Cold War concerns of the narrative contain not only a fable for our time, but the echoes of a more ancient myth.

Aldrich's approach to *Kiss Me Deadly*'s brutality is, for him, elegant to the point of fastidiousness (almost as though he were distancing himself and the audience from the film's New York and Los Angeles wastelands) which seems as negative of real emotion as though an atom bomb had already scoured the world. The nuclear hysteria that raged at the time of the film's production is transmuted by the director into powerful deterministic comment.

What begins as a sordid story of underworld intrigue, conspiracy and the search for what is called 'the great whatsit', assumes the irrational nature of nightmare. And there are so many subjective shots from Hammer's point of view – notably when knocked out from behind, and when he is about to open the locker that supposedly contains the answer to all mysteries – that it is evident that, though disclaimed, he is the figure with whom the audience identifies. What he does, he does in our name. As political comment then, *Kiss Me Deadly* daringly persuades its audience – and in 1955, a year of Cold War, it *was* daring – that legalized

thugs like Hammer could hamfistedly seek out radioactivity, leading to climactic destruction. That he was led to it by a woman, Lily Carver, is just another aspect of an ignorant gullibility that is as much part of his sexual nature as his intellect. Ignorance undoes all things; even, in opening the ultimate box, mankind.

Ralph Meeker's performance as Hammer never concedes the slightest shred of decency, as though the actor heroically realized that a one-dimensional character is the only way to set into more defined relief the other perspectives of situation and character. Its connections with the Lemmy Caution of Jean-Luc Godard's *Alphaville*, made ten years afterwards, are only too apparent.

In his book *Film Noir*, Alain Silver has written:

'What distinguishes *Kiss Me Deadly*'s figurative usage from that of other Aldrich films is an explicit

aural fabric of allusions and metaphor: the recurring Christina Rossetti poem, *Remember Me*; the Caruso recording . . . they all provide immediate textual reference if not subsidiary meaning.'

Accordingly, and with its necessary undertow of credibility, *Kiss Me Deadly* provides a suitable, realistic context for an allegory – and the film is all the more disturbing in that it is really communicating about the nuclear age in ancient legend. For as Lily Carver opens the box and becomes a column of fire – a pillar of salt? – and Hammer and Velda look backwards from the sea to watch the house mushroom upwards into devastation, so the audience realizes just what has been unleashed by all their separate actions. The totem-words of nuclear armament have already been uttered: 'Manhattan project . . . Los Alamos . . . Trinity'.

The word that is never said, but that is most implicit in all that hap-

pens, is Pandora. It is her box that has been breached. The breaking of encasing restraint, the unleashing of the apocalypse, is what those Hammer-blows have achieved. It is more than enough.

TOM HUTCHINSON

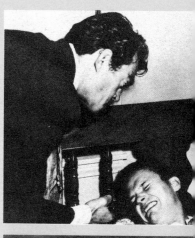

Directed by Robert Aldrich, 1955
Prod co: Parklane Pictures (United Artists). **exec prod:** Victor Saville. **prod:** Robert Aldrich. **sc:** A. I. Bezzerides, from the novel by Mickey Spillane. **photo:** Ernest Laszlo. **ed:** Michael Luciano. **art dir:** William Glasgow. **mus:** Frank DeVol. **song:** 'Rather Have the Blues' by Frank DeVol, sung by Nat 'King' Cole. **ass dir:** Robert Justman. **r/t:** 96 minutes.
Cast: Ralph Meeker (*Mike Hammer*), Albert Dekker (*Dr Soberin*), Paul Stewart (*Carl Evello*), Maxine Cooper (*Velda*), Gaby Rodgers (*Gabrielle/Lily Carver*), Wesley Addy (*Pat*), Juano Hernandez (*Eddie Eager*), Nick Dennis (*Nick*), Cloris Leachman (*Christina*), Marian Carr (*Friday*), Jack Lambert (*Sugar*), Jack Elam (*Charlie Max*), Jerry Zinneman (*Sammy*), Percy Helton (*morgue doctor*), Fortunio Bonanova (*Carmen Trivago*), Silvio Minciotti (*mover*), Leigh Snowden (*girl at pool*), Madi Comfort (*singer*), James Seay, Robert Cornthwaite (*FBI men*), Mara McAfee (*nurse*), James McCallian (*'Super'*), Jesslyn Fax (*Mrs 'Super'*), Mort Marshall (*Piker*), Strother Martin (*truck driver*), Marjorie Bennett (*manager*), Art Loggins (*bartender*), Bob Sherman (*gas-station man*), Keith McConnell (*athletic-club clerk*), Paul Richards (*attacker*).

5

32

1

2

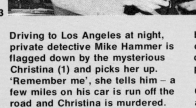

3

4

Driving to Los Angeles at night, private detective Mike Hammer is flagged down by the mysterious Christina (1) and picks her up. 'Remember me', she tells him – a few miles on his car is run off the road and Christina is murdered.

Hammer wakes in hospital where his secretary Velda and a colleague tell him (2) that federal investigators want to question him about Christina. A conspiracy led by gangster Carl Evello tries to

buy Hammer off with the gift of a car, but he and his mechanic Nick discover in time that it has been planted with explosives (3).

Hammer seeks out Lily Carver, Christina's former room-mate, and takes her to his apartment. Shortly afterwards Nick is murdered and Hammer abducted by Evello's hired thugs (4). They take him to Dr Soberin – Christina's killer – who has him restrained (5) and injects him with

pentathol. But Hammer kills one of the heavies and escapes.

Velda has disappeared. But with the help of Lily Carver Hammer decodes Christina's message. It leads them to a morgue where a doctor passes on the key to a locker (6) containing a box. Hammer leaves the box there; Lily meanwhile has gone.

At his apartment the police tell Hammer the box contains radioactive material sought by

foreign agents. Finding the locker empty, Hammer gets Soberin's address off one of his patients' medicine bottles (7). At his beach house, Lily kills the doctor to get the box for herself (8) and shoots and wounds Hammer when he arrives. She opens the box, engulfing herself in flames (9) and starting a nuclear chain reaction. Hammer finds Velda and they stumble into the sea (10) as the house explodes.

6

7

9

10

THE END

A PARKLANE PICTURE
RELEASED THROUGH UNITED ARTISTS

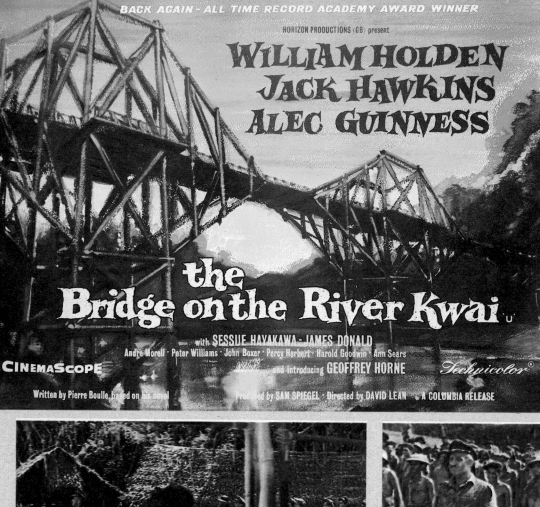

BACK AGAIN - ALL TIME RECORD ACADEMY AWARD WINNER

HORIZON PRODUCTIONS (GB) present

WILLIAM HOLDEN
JACK HAWKINS
ALEC GUINNESS

the Bridge on the River Kwai U

with SESSUE HAYAKAWA · JAMES DONALD

André Morell · Peter Williams · John Boxer · Percy Herbert · Harold Goodwin · Ann Sears
and introducing GEOFFREY HORNE

CINEMASCOPE
Technicolor

Written by Pierre Boulle, based on his novel   Produced by SAM SPIEGEL · Directed by DAVID LEAN · A COLUMBIA RELEASE

The film that 'achieved the rarity of bringing back the long queues outside every cinema at which it was shown', that was how *Film Review* in 1959 looked back on the success of *The Bridge on the River Kwai*. Audiences were drawn to it because it moved away from the, by now clichéd, World War II film which was full of blood and thunder, concentrating instead on the psychological battle between two of its main characters. It was also the first of David Lean's super-productions, setting the pattern for his subsequent films – *Lawrence of Arabia* (1962), *Doctor Zhivago* (1965) and *Ryan's Daughter* (1970). The film was shot largely on location in Ceylon, cost over $3 million and took over a year to make. *The Bridge on the River Kwai* became the first British film to win an Academy Award for Best Film, and it earned its makers another six Oscars, including those for Best Actor (Alec Guinness), Best Director and Best Screenplay.

In a prisoner-of-war camp in Siam, the English Colonel Nicholson and the Japanese Colonel Saito confront each other as prisoner and warden. Since they have a common profession and rank, their differen-

2

Directed by David Lean, 1957

Prod co: Horizon Pictures. **prod:** Sam Spiegel. **sc:** Pierre Boulle, from his own novel. **photo** (CinemaScope, Technicolor): Jack Hildyard. **ed:** Peter Taylor. **art dir:** Donald M. Ashton. **sd:** John Cox, John Mitchell. **mus:** Malcolm Arnold. **r/t:** 161 minutes.
Cast: William Holden (*Shears*), Alec Guinness (*Colonel Nicholson*), Jack Hawkins (*Major Warden*), Sessue Hayakawa (*Colonel Saito*), James Donald (*Doctor Clipton*), Geoffrey Horne (*Lieutenant Joyce*), André Morell (*Colonel Green*), Peter Williams (*Captain Reeves*), John Boxer (*Major Hughes*), Percy Herbert (*Grogan*), Harold Goodwin (*Baker*), Ann Sears (*nurse*), Henry Okawa (*Captain Kanematsu*), K. Katsumoto (*Lieutenant Miura*), M. R. B. Chakrabandhu (*Yai*), Vilaiwan Seeboonreaung, Ngamta Suphaphongs, Javanart Punynchoti (*Siamese girls*).

5

English prisoners-of-war arrive at a Japanese camp in Siam (1), where they are commanded by Colonel Saito to build a bridge as one link in the notorious death railway. Colonel Nicholson, the English commander, refuses to cooperate when Saito orders the officers to work alongside the enlisted men, as it breaks the Geneva Convention. Nicholson keeps his men standing in the hot sun all day (2) rather than give the order to begin work. Saito arrests Nicholson and throws him into the sweat-box (3).

Using the anniversary of an ancient Japanese victory as an excuse. They come to an agreement (4) whereby the officers are allowed to supervise the construction of the bridge (5). Nicholson, in order to maintain the men's morale, begins to direct operations so as to make the bridge a lasting tribute to the efficiency of the British soldier. He becomes obsessed with the job even though, in so doing, he is helping the Japanese war effort.

Meanwhile, an American named Shears has escaped from the camp. He seeks refuge in a local village where he is helped by a young girl. When he eventually gets back to headquarters, hoping to go home, he is ordered against his will by Major Warden to join an allied raid to destroy the bridge. He returns to the river Kwai (6), with Warden, to carry out this mission.

After a camp concert to celebrate the completion of the bridge (7), Nicholson inspects his work and sees the dynamite leads that Shears and his fellow commandos have laid (8). Alerting Saito to the danger of sabotage, he follows the leads to investigate their origin. In the fight that follows (9), Nicholson and Saito are all killed, but Nicholson falls on the detonator and blows up the bridge at the exact moment when a supply train is passing over it.

Clipton, the British doctor of the camp, watching the scene in horror utters despairingly: 'Madness, madness'.

34

ces are in some ways superficial. They share a deep commitment to the belief that only their own side can provide a civilized basis for humanity. In addition, they each have their own orders which they are determined to obey to the letter. Saito's, from the Imperial Command, instruct him to build a bridge over the River Kwai to provide a crucial link for men and supplies in Japanese military operations. Nicholson's orders derive from the Geneva Convention governing the conditions and treatment of prisoners-of-war – rules that may hinder the building of the bridge. Both men also represent a different code of behaviour. Nicholson's is that of the English gentleman: 'Without law there is no civilization', he tells Saito. He thus stoically suffers torture to defend the principle that officers will not work alongside enlisted men. However he has an overriding faith in the quality of English workmanship and the endurance of the British soldier. After all, the British, he believes, were able to create their empire because of their technical and moral superiority.

Saito's code is that of the Japanese warrior – *bushido*. At the beginning of the film he is shown wearing the traditional Japanese kimono, and he keeps his ceremonial sword with him at all times. He despises the English because, as he tells Nicholson, 'You are defeated but you have no shame'. When he publicly loses face, he knows that in the end his only recourse will be suicide by his own sword.

Lean deliberately distances the audience from this central conflict by upsetting the usual balance of sympathy. Saito is not the traditional 'baddie' of many war films, and Nicholson is not the usual heroic representative of the British war effort. Sam Spiegel, the film's producer, commented:

'The day of the dark, dog-kicking villain is gone and in his place has come the heavy whom audiences can understand and with whom they can sympathize.'

In contrast to Nicholson and Saito, the American Shears is not governed by an inflexible code or blinkered by patriotism. As Saito and Nicholson grow to understand and respect each other's differences, they appear to merge their identities; Shears, good-humoured and enterprising, is somewhat different. For him war is not a heroic 'game' but simply a question of survival. In the camp, he lies about his rank in order to get the preferential treatment reserved for officers and he disobeys Nicholson's orders by escaping. Having reached safety, he only undertakes the perilous commando raid on the bridge with the utmost reluctance. He is in many ways a typical Hollywood hero in the self-reliant 'Bogart' tradition.

Having built the bridge, Nicholson nearly succeeds in thwarting an Allied commando raid to destroy it. His commitment to his code has resulted in the betrayal of his own side. The doctor, who functions as a neutral observer throughout the film, sums up Nicholson's determination to build the bridge when he exclaims 'Madness, madness' – a comment on the war as much as on Nicholson. To quote Spiegel again:

'Man came into the world to build and not to destroy. Yet he's thrown into the necessity of destroying, and his everlasting instinct is to try to save himself from having to destroy.'

When making the film, the production team had great difficulty both in building the bridge and in blowing it up. It was constructed of logs moved into position by elephants and teams of men and at the time was the largest film set ever built. Hollywood methods proved incapable of blowing up the bridge with the train running across it, and so a team of experts from Ceylon's Imperial Chemical Industries was brought in to advise. Even then it took several attempts before the blast could be set off at exactly the right time. The train was driven by a stunt man across the bridge. When it was a quarter of the way across, he had to swing out of the cab and race back, hidden from the cameras, only seconds before the dynamite was detonated. The last coach on the train carried more dynamite, which was primed to explode when that coach hit the bottom of the ravine. The result is one of the most spectacular explosions ever seen on the screen.

In the book on which the film was based, the bridge is left standing as a symbol of the futility of war. Lean's decision to destroy the bridge transfers attention to the contradictions within Nicholson's attitude, and the perils of a blind commitment to any code.

SALLY HIBBIN

3

4

6

7

8

9

M·G·M presents

CARY GRANT
EVA MARIE SAINT
JAMES MASON

ALFRED HITCHCOCK'S

NORTH BY NORTHWEST

VISTAVISION
TECHNICOLOR®

Co-starring JESSIE ROYCE LANDIS
Written by ERNEST LEHMAN · Directed by ALFRED HITCHCOCK

AN M-G-M PICTURE

1

3

5

North by Northwest was greeted with sighs of pleasure and relief by those numerous admirers of Hitchcock who were perplexed by the romantic obsession of *Vertigo* (1958). Following *North by Northwest*, Hitchcock made *Psycho* (1960) and viewers were again confronted by a work they did not quite know how to take – as Gothic extravagance, as black comedy or as an appalling lapse of taste.

Superficially, *North by Northwest* is a *divertissement* between two emotionally disturbing films, a colourful spy frolic starring the amiable Cary Grant; a chase movie told with a gleeful disregard for plot but with immense professional skill and good humour. But the film, which Hitchcock described as the culmination of his work in America, contains many darker elements within its genre framework that place it alongside *Vertigo* and *Psycho* as a comment on the char-

acter of American society.

The project came about by chance. Before shooting began on *Vertigo*, Hitchcock was hired by MGM to direct *The Wreck of the Mary Deare* to which screenwriter Ernest Lehman was also assigned. Both men soon realized the problems in adapting Hammond Innes' novel. They began instead on an original story, a spy thriller, which apparently started with Hitchcock's wish to film a sequence on Mount Rushmore. *The Man on Lincoln's Nose* was an early title and Hitchcock conceived an irreverent scene (never shot) in which the hero hides in one of Lincoln's nostrils and gets a sneezing fit.

In the initial stages of preparation it was intended as a James Stewart film but as the main character developed it became a Cary Grant film. This is a crucial element in the film's well-oiled mechanism. Whereas Stewart's persona is one

7

8

9

of integrity and dedication to cause, Grant's is one of cynicism, independence and flamboyance.

Grant's Roger Thornhill is the classic adman: smart and shallow, a believer only in himself, unshakably complacent, unattached and on the make. His personalized bookmatches, inscribed with the initials R.O.T., emphasize the zero in his life. The film charts a moral and spiritual growth by stripping away what identity he has and by forcing him to adopt the identity of someone who does not exist.

Thornhill's commitment at the end is not to the ideals of America, as embodied by the paternalistic head of the CIA (Thornhill already has a dominant mother who keeps a check on his drinking), but to Eve Kendall, another in his long line of women. The survival of this species of American male is a dispiriting prospect just off the edges of the frame.

The opening scenes establish Thornhill as being master of his environment – his ease at commandeering someone else's cab; his relaxed charm in smart cocktail bars. Thornhill is every inch the American man-about-town and, appropriately, it is a man called Townsend who propels him from New York into a world of chaos.

The plot's physical and spiritual trajectory is a north-westerly one

and a historical one, with Vandamm's Old World suavity adding a cultural perspective to this satire of the New World. From New York's Plaza Hotel and United Nations building (symbols, respectively, of material success and Utopia) we travel on the *Twentieth Century* to Chicago, with its memories of gangsters (now the CIA and spies). The justly celebrated cropduster sequence, when Thornhill is attacked by the swooping plane, takes place on the wide prairie complete with farmers who might have stepped out of the pages of John Steinbeck. Mount Rushmore's presidents carved in stone is the ultimate symbol of order and tolerance but is used as the setting for betrayals, homosexual jealousies (Vandamm's sadistic henchman) and violence. The American Dream has turned into a horrifying nightmare.

Against this is a palpable background of moral ambiguity and world tension – 'Trouble in the Middle East', cries a prescient New York newsboy. Hitchcock's slow dissolve from the violated United Nations building to the bronze CIA plaque seems now to encompass the cynicism of the Seventies and Eighties and perhaps should not be taken as lightly as Thornhill's flip comment early in the film, 'This is ridiculous'. ADRIAN TURNER

Directed by Alfred Hitchcock, 1959
Prod co: Alfred Hitchcock/MGM. **prod:** Alfred Hitchcock. **assoc prod:** Herbert Coleman. **sc:** Ernest Lehman. **photo** (Technicolor, VistaVision): Robert Burks. **sp eff:** A. Arnold Gillespie, Lee LeBlanc. **art dir:** Robert Boyle, William A. Horning. **mus:** Bernard Herrmann. **sd:** Frank Milton. **ed:** George Tomasini. **titles:** Saul Bass. **r/t:** 136 minutes.
Cast: Cary Grant (*Roger Thornhill*), Eva-Marie Saint (*Eve Kendall*), James Mason (*Phillip Vandamm*), Jessie Royce Landis (*Clara Thornhill*), Leo G. Carroll (*The Professor*), Philip Ober (*Lester Townsend*), Josephine Hutchinson (*Mrs Townsend*), Martin Landau (*Leonard*), Adam Williams (*Valerian*).

Roger Thornhill, a New York advertising executive, is kidnapped in the Plaza Hotel and taken to see Phillip Vandamm (1), a spy dealing in American secrets who has briefly taken over the home of Townsend, a diplomat. Vandamm believes Thornhill is George Kaplan, a CIA agent, and forces him to drink a bottle of bourbon before putting him blind-drunk in a car.

Instead of crashing as planned, Thornhill is arrested (2) for drunken driving but is released on bail through the charm of his doting mother. Following a clue found in Kaplan's hotel room, Thornhill goes to the United Nations building. He meets Townsend who suddenly falls dead with a knife in his back (3).

Now a prime murder suspect, Thornhill boards a train for Chicago where Kaplan has gone. On the train he meets Eve Kendall (4) who helps him evade the police and arranges a meeting with Kaplan on the open prairie. Whilst Thornhill waits for Kaplan (5), a crop-dusting plane attacks him (6) but Thornhill narrowly escapes and the plane

crashes into a passing vehicle (7).

He tracks Eve down to an art auction where she sits with Vandamm. Feeling threatened once more, Thornhill ingeniously escapes by getting himself arrested but this time The Professor, of the CIA, intervenes, explaining that Kaplan is an imaginary agent designed to divert Vandamm's attention away from the real CIA agent, Eve, whose cover Thornhill has virtually blown.

Thornhill flies to Mount Rushmore where, as part of a plan, Eve shoots him with blanks (8) to reassure the suspicious and jealous Vandamm. Thornhill later meets Eve and learns that her duty demands that she leave America with Vandamm. Disobeying orders, Thornhill rescues Eve from Vandamm, who had intended killing her. They nearly fall to their deaths from Mount Rushmore (9) before The Professor's men arrest Vandamm and kill his henchmen.

The microfilm Vandamm was to deliver to the enemy is saved and Thornhill and Eve return to New York by train (10).

Rio Bravo has come to be accepted as a perfect example both of the Western genre and of the work of its director, Howard Hawks. It was not born with that reputation. 'Well-made but awfully familiar fare', declared A. H. Weiler in the *New York Times*. 'The film lasts almost as long as five TV Westerns laid end to end', drawled *Time* magazine. Arthur Knight in *The Saturday Review* saw further:

'As standard Western fare as has ever turned up on a Hollywood menu . . . But when brewed by Howard Hawks . . . suddenly everything begins to work. There is excitement, tension, the pleasure of looking at Western landscapes, and the age-old justification when the good guys beat the bad . . .'

It was nearly three years after the failure of his *Land of the Pharaohs* (1955) that Hawks resumed his career with *Rio Bravo*, shooting it in May–July 1958 with Old Tucson, Arizona, as the main location. Hawks decided to 'try and get a little of the spirit we used to make pictures with'; he was inspired, in a backhanded way, by Fred Zinnemann's *High Noon* (1952) which concerned a marshal confronted by revenge-seeking desperadoes. As Hawks noted in an interview with Peter Bogdanovich:

'Gary Cooper ran around trying to get help and no one would give him any. And that's rather a silly thing for a man to do, especially since at the end of the picture he is able to do the job by himself. So I said, we'll do just the opposite, and take a real professional viewpoint: as Wayne says when he's offered help, "If they're really good, I'll take them. If not, I'll just have to take care of them".'

High Noon may not have been the only Western that influenced Hawks. The central situation of a lawman holding a prisoner under siege had occurred strikingly in *3.10 to Yuma* (1957) and Walter Brennan had played a jail-keeper in another good Western, *The Proud Ones* (1956) which, like *Rio Bravo*, concerned the relationship between a marshal and his deputy.

However, Hawks deliberately emphasized characterization over plot in making *Rio Bravo*. He realized that television series had made most Western plots excessively familiar. Rather audaciously, Hawks and his screenwriters, Jules Furthman and Leigh Brackett, did little to develop the personalities of the villains, who were normally more colourful and extravagant than the heroes of Fifties Westerns – for instance, Jack Palance in *Shane* (1953). The prisoner, played by Claude Akins, is adequately established but not dwelt upon; and the men outside are even less individualized, notable only for their number. Instead, Hawks makes his key relationship that between John Wayne as sheriff and Dean Martin as the alcoholic deputy. The deputy's full recovery of self-esteem is the main story development. The old jail-keeper and the young gunhand played by Ricky Nelson complete a group united in their professionalism and loyalty towards each other. In this respect, the film recalls Hawks' *Only Angels Have Wings* (1939), scripted by Jules Furthman, about a group of flyers whom Cary Grant, as their leader, keeps on a steady course.

Furthman also worked on Josef von Sternberg's *Underworld* (1927) with its provocative gangster's moll called 'Feathers'; the character of the same name played by Angie Dickinson in *Rio Bravo* is initially viewed as a distraction but proves her worth. Even in the somewhat suspect casting of pop singer Ricky Nelson, Hawks not only allowed him to sing but found a use for it when the others in the group join in the song – or, in Wayne's case, observe benevolently – as an expression of team solidarity.

Hawks himself explained another way in which the relationships were subtly developed:

'Dean Martin had a bit in which he was required to roll a cigarette. His fingers weren't equal to it and Wayne kept passing him cigarettes. All of a sudden you realize that they are awfully good friends or he wouldn't be doing it.'

This was a piece of business worked out on the set.

The film was a comfortable success, revitalizing Hawks' career, although ten other 1959 releases did better on the North American market and it came out level at the box-office with Fred Zinnemann's *The Nun's Story*. Hawks continued to make films in similar vein, stronger on characters than in story. In *El Dorado* (1967) and *Rio Lobo* (1970) he even re-used the format of *Rio Bravo*, but with diminishing results.

Rio Bravo also influenced young film-makers, notably John Carpenter who updated its basic situation into a modern-day Los Angeles police station under siege in *Assault on Precinct 13* (1976) and acknowledged his indebtedness by editing the film under the pseudonym of 'John T. Chance', the name of the sheriff played by Wayne in *Rio Bravo*.
ALLEN EYLES

Directed by Howard Hawks, 1959
Prod co: Armada. **prod:** Howard Hawks. **sc:** Jules Furthman, Leigh Brackett, from a story by B. H. McCampbell. **photo** (Technicolor): Russell Harlan. **ed:** Folmar Blangsted. **art dir:** Leo K. Kuter. **cost:** Marjorie Best. **mus:** Dmitri Tiomkin. **lyr:** Paul Francis Webster. **sd:** Robert B. Lee. **ass dir:** Paul Helmick. **r/t:** 141 minutes.
Cast: John Wayne (*John T. Chance*), Dean Martin (*Dude*), Ricky Nelson (*Colorado Ryan*), Ward Bond (*Pat Wheeler*), Angie Dickinson (*Feathers*), Walter Brennan (*Stumpy*), John Russell (*Nathan Burdett*), Pedro Gonzalez-Gonzalez (*Carlos*), Estelita Rodriguez (*Consuela*), Claude Akins (*Joe Burdett*), Malcolm Atterbury (*Jake*), Harry Carey Jr (*Harold*), Bob Steele (*Matt Harris*), Bob Terhune (*bartender*), Ted White (*Bart*).

Dude, a former deputy in the Texas border town of Rio Bravo, has been disappointed in love and turns to drink, becoming the town's laughing-stock (1). He pulls himself together to help sheriff John T. Chance in arresting Joe Burdett for murder and gets another crack at his old job (2).

Joe's rancher brother, Nathan, bottles the town up tight while the cantankerous jail-keeper Stumpy (3) is ready to shoot Joe if any rescue attempt is made. Chance tries to order a gambling woman, Feathers, to leave town but she stays and befriends him (4). Chance's old friend Pat Wheeler arrives in town (5), offers help and is gunned down by Nathan's men. Chance is taken by surprise on Main Street and rescued by Feathers and by Colorado, Wheeler's young gunhand (6), who becomes a deputy (7). Dude is captured by Nathan Burdett and Chance agrees to a trade. But Dude leaps on Joe as they pass each other in the exchange and the two sides shoot it out.

Chance's team uses dynamite to blast the Burdett gang into surrender (8). Feathers puts on her scanty saloon-hostess costume (9), provoking Chance into declaring his love for her by forbidding her to appear like that in public.

1

2

3

4

5

8

9

PSYCHO

Directed by Alfred Hitchcock, 1960

Prod co: Shamley (Paramount). **prod:** Alfred Hitchcock. **sc:** Joseph Stefano, from a novel by Robert Bloch. **titles:** Saul Bass. **photo:** John L. Russell. **sp eff photo:** Clarence Champagne. **ed:** George Tomasini. **art dir:** Joseph Hurley, Robert Clatworthy, George Milo. **mus:** Bernard Herrmann. **sd rec:** Walden O. Watson, William Russell. **r/t:** 108 minutes.
Cast: Anthony Perkins (*Norman Bates*), John Gavin (*Sam Loomis*), Janet Leigh (*Marion Crane*), Vera Miles (*Lila Crane*), John McIntyre (*Sheriff Chambers*), Martin Balsam (*Milton Arbogast*), Simon Oakland (*Dr Richmond*).

'For all the fake intimacy of the opening love scene and the manifest absurdity of the denouement, *Psycho* comes nearer to attaining an exhilarating balance between content and style than anything Hitchcock has done in years. Of course, it is a very minor work.'

This remarkable statement is taken from Peter John Dyer's review in *Sight and Sound* (Autumn 1960). Later in the same piece Dyer asserted that 'Hitchcock is not a serious director (except in his worst films)' and that *Psycho* has 'an unacceptable basic premise' but offers a high degree of 'craftsmanship'. In other words, it is a tasteless and cynical tale well told.

This review seems extraordinary today but it speaks volumes about critical priorities in 1960 when a film could be grudgingly and guiltily praised for technical excellence but haughtily dismissed on moral grounds. Serious directors were not allowed to dabble with genre material such as horror. The fact that *Psycho* is as complex and as challenging as Antonioni's *L'Avventura* (1960, *The Adventure*)

and Resnais' *L'Année Dernière à Marienbad* (1961, *Last Year in Marienbad*) – two notably Hitchcockian films of the same period – would not have occurred to most critics of the time for whom Westerns and melodramas represented the most blatant commercialism. Michael Powell's *Peeping Tom* (1960), a blood-brother of *Psycho*, was greeted with even more critical scorn.

Happily, the critical climate changed in the Sixties and many of the major battles were fought over Hitchcock's work in general and *Psycho* in particular – its box-office success had turned it into a social phenomenon. The film's importance is now acknowledged and it has influenced a wide range of film-makers. Audiences, too, have been conditioned by *Psycho* to recognize the strategies at work in such films.

Psycho is a comparative rarity among horror films in that repeated viewings do not diminish its power; indeed, as the characters become more and more familiar each time the film is seen, so the viewer's unease and apprehension grow. **6**

Hitchcock himself has defined this as a response to 'pure film'. In the sense that 'pure film' implies more than 'craftsmanship', *Psycho* is perhaps the most detailed and rigorously constructed of Hitchcock's films. Its continuing fascination and power to involve (not to say enslave) its audience is also because *Psycho* is neither a whodunnit (Hitchcock was never interested in those) nor a conventional thriller (there is no hero); instead, it is an essay on the universality of evil in which the audience plays the most significant role. It is an appeal to and a criticism of the film audience's voyeuristic impulses and the cinematic apparatus.

Norman Bates' schizophrenia becomes the audience's, just as the audience is implicated in Marion Crane's submission to crime. At first the viewer identifies with Marion, sharing her panic when she encounters the traffic cop and understanding her irrational behaviour at the gas station. And after her decision to return the money,

her shower washes away her guilt – and that of everyone watching. Then comes the murder, and interest switches to Norman, culminating in the moment when Marion's car refuses to sink into the swamp. The sigh of relief, and then the grin that passes across Norman's face when the car finally does sink, again implicates 'the watcher' in his diabolism. Then Arbogast the detective, and then Sam and Lila become the focus for audience sympathy. The setting is equally schizoid – a Gothic gingerbread house and a banal modern motel.

The insistent mirror imagery emphasizes the theme and also alerts the audience to the characters and the actors playing them. Norman cares for his mother; Sam, apparently, is paying alimony and the debts of his dead father; Marion's office colleague has a prying mother; the rich businessman is a domineering father; the woman in Sam's hardware store is possibly buying insecticide to kill her husband; Marion's apartment is decorated with family photographs; and Lila has assumed the role of Marion's mother. Everyone talks incessantly about murder and family strife and Norman and Sam, and Marion and Lila, are even mirror images of each other.

This strategy creates an oppressive world from which escape is impossible (the audience is hooked). The suffocating bird imagery – Norman's stuffed birds, his mummified mother, Marion's surname, the city of Phoenix – suggests predestination, as does the license plate of Marion's last car, bearing the initials of Norman Bates, and Marion and Sam's early dialogue about the ignominy of hotel rooms.

For 108 minutes *Psycho* perforates the viewer's belief in the icons of the capitalist dream – money, family, sex – and analyses his demons instead. The film's abrasive wit prevents a total descent into the heart of darkness, while its effectiveness gains considerably from Bernard Herrmann's music and Anthony Perkins' performance which ranks with the finest the cinema has to offer. ADRIAN TURNER

After spending the lunch-hour in a hotel room with her lover Sam (1), Marion Crane returns to work. Her boss (2) entrusts her with $40,000 in cash but Marion goes home, packs a bag, and leaves town. She sleeps in her car and is woken by a cop who follows her to a garage where, using some of the stolen money, she changes cars. That night she stays at the Bates Motel and chats with the manager, Norman (3), who looks after his sick mother in the nearby house (4). Marion takes a shower and is stabbed to death (5). Norman, blaming his mother, cleans up the mess, puts the body into Marion's own car and drives it into a swamp (6).

Marion's sister Lila visits Sam and they are joined by Arbogast, a private detective. Arbogast checks hotels, interviews Norman (7) and is murdered when he returns to see Mrs Bates. Sam and Lila check into the motel and Sam keeps Norman talking while Lila (8) searches the house. Sensing trouble, Norman knocks Sam unconscious. Lila enters the cellar (9) and finds the clothed skeleton of Mrs Bates.

The ending? Hitchcock would turn in his grave if we told . . .

1

2

3

4

5

8

9

The *Manchurian Candidate* was acclaimed as an outstanding political thriller but it was not taken particularly seriously when it first appeared. Frank Sinatra's box-office popularity enabled it to draw good audiences despite its complex style and unusual narrative. The film was a close adaptation of Richard Condon's 1959 novel, prepared by John Frankenheimer and George Axelrod as an independent production, refused by major studios until Sinatra wanted to star in it, then economically shot in 39 days.

It was the first film to directly criticize the McCarthy era. Senator John Iselin in the film is a loud-mouthed super-patriot who accuses the Secretary of Defence of harbouring Communists in his department but has difficulty in alleging a consistent number of them. Shaking out Heinz tomato ketchup onto his food, he decides there are 57 Communists, the same number as there are Heinz varieties. But even more outrageous than the buffoonish depiction of Iselin was the suggestion that this kind of man made an ideal dupe for the Communists, just the kind of President they could easily manipulate in the White House.

'If you come in five minutes after this picture begins, you won't know what it's all about!' warned the advertisements, referring to the ingenious handling of the Manchurian sequence. In this the friendly Chinese lecturer, demonstrating the hold he has over the captured soldiers' minds, is seen by the men in their brainwashed state as a Southern lady in an ornate hotel setting giving a boring lecture on hydrangeas (the Negro soldier sees him as a black woman) and the camera pans round the hall between the actual speaker and the one imagined by the captives. The strangling and shooting of two soldiers by the programmed Raymond Shaw is then done with the calm co-operation and mild interest of the men – a chilling demonstration of the power of brainwashing, and one that is necessary to make the audience accept what will later unfold.

Laurence Harvey was cleverly cast as Shaw. His cold, arrogant screen persona ideally suited a man who knows he is almost unlovable and is therefore all the more tragic when he is forced to kill the few people who have treated him well: his best friend in Manchuria, his wife and his father-in-law.

'To make this wild plot believable – and I want people to believe it and take it seriously – every scene had to be done with the utmost reality and clarity', recalled Frankenheimer. Yet at the same time the director ingeniously heightened the effect of some scenes by the way he shot them. Television monitors multiply the sense of confusion and contradiction as Iselin interrupts the Secretary of Defense's press conference with his woolly accusations. When Raymond Shaw is accidentally triggered off to obey the remark 'Go jump in a lake', the absurdity of his actions is further

You must not miss the first five minutes to know what it's all about!

Frank Sinatra

when you've seen it all, you'll swear there's never been anything like it!

Laurence Harvey

Janet Leigh

The Manchurian Candidate A

co-starring Angela Lansbury · Henry Silva · James Gregory Produced by GEORGE AXELROD and JOHN FRANKENHEIMER

Directed by JOHN FRANKENHEIMER Screenplay by GEORGE AXELROD Based upon a Novel by RICHARD CONDON Executive Producer HOWARD W. KOCH An M. C. PRODUCTION UNITED ARTISTS

The Manchurian Candidate

compounded by the time he takes to get to a lake and by the water being frozen over. Shaw's approach to it is shot through a long lens that slows him down and makes him look appropriately mechanical as well as hiding the lake from view until he jumps into it. The plump, Dickensian Senator Jordan is shot standing defenceless in a dressing-gown, and the bullet passes through a milk carton in his hand, the contents streaming out in a graphic substitution for blood.

The film also offers the ultimate portrait of smothering American momism. Angela Lansbury, as Shaw's mother, is the literal 'Red Queen' – the agent who controls her son as a puppet through the Queen of Diamonds playing card. Her truly monstrous figure is contrasted with Janet Leigh's Rosie, again strong-willed but considerate. Her romance with Sinatra's Bennett Marco is conducted on Hawksian lines: she makes the running and comforts the deeply troubled man, bailing him out of jail as though she has known him for years. In Condon's book, Rosie was described as Arabic-looking; the film has Marco ask Rosie 'Are you Arabic?', a much-quoted line that no longer fits yet adds to the absurd flavour, her denial allowing Marco to rephrase the question, 'Put it another way – are you married?', and get at the spontaneous attraction between them.

Criticism was directed at the film's coda in which Marco praises Shaw's courage in shooting himself

Directed by John Frankenheimer, 1962.
Prod co: M. C. **prod:** George Axelrod, John Frankenheimer. **sc:** George Axelrod, from the novel by Richard Condon. **photo:** Lionel Lindon. **ed:** Ferris Webster. **art dir:** Richard Sylbert. **cost:** Moss Mabry. **mus:** David Amram. **sd:** Joe Edmondson. **ass dir:** Joseph Behm. **r/t:** 126 minutes.
Cast: Frank Sinatra (*Bennett Marco*), Laurence Harvey (*Raymond Shaw*), Janet Leigh (*Rosie*), Angela Lansbury (*Raymond's mother*), Henry Silva (*Chunjin*), James Gregory (*Senator John Iselin*), Leslie Parrish (*Jocie Jordon*), John McGiver (*Senator Thomas Jordon*), Khigh Dhiegh (*Yen Lo*), James Edwards (*Corporal Melvin*), Douglas Henderson (*Colonel*), Albert Paulsen (*Zilkov*), Barry Kelley (*Secretary of Defense*), Lloyd Corrigan (*Holborn Gaines*), Madame Spivy (*Berezovo's lady counterpart*), Joe Adams (*psychiatrist*), Whit Bissell (*medical officer*).

and his manipulators: it may have been devised to give its major star the last word, but it does point up Shaw's real act of valour compared to that with which he was credited by the brainwashed patrol at the start of the film. This is the major change from the novel, where Shaw's final acts were still not his own but ordered by Marco.

With the Kennedy assassinations, the Watergate affair and the arrival of Ronald Reagan in the White House, *The Manchurian Candidate* no longer seems as fanciful as it did to contemporary critics who admired its ingenuity and imagination. Arthur Knight, in *The Saturday Review* saw it as an updated Fu Manchu melodrama, noting:

'It is always disturbing when melodrama plays fast and loose with serious, even incendiary material' and concluding, 'It is the best-told story of the year... it is also the most irresponsible.'

It was temporarily withdrawn from circulation after President Kennedy's assassination amid conjecture that it might have planted the idea for the murder. Later, Frankenheimer a close friend of Robert Kennedy, drove him to the hotel on the evening he was killed. 'I find it impossible to become involved in politics since his death'. Frankenheimer has said, declining the chance to direct *Executive Action* (1973), which explored the conspiracy theory of John F. Kennedy's assassination.

Variety predicted that *The Manchurian Candidate* would win many Oscars but it was obviously too challenging for the Hollywood community. *Lawrence of Arabia, The Miracle Worker* and *To Kill a Mockingbird* (all 1962) dominated the Awards – all films safely set in the past. Only Angela Lansbury and Ferris Webster, the film's editor, were nominated and neither won.

ALLEN EYLES

An American army patrol is captured by Chinese Communists in Korea and taken to Manchuria. The men are brainwashed into watching impassively as one of their number, Raymond Shaw, who has been programmed to kill in response to a 'trigger' sign, is tested and kills two of his comrades (1). All the men, including Shaw, are made to believe they have completed a successful mission before they are returned to their own side.

Back in America, one of the patrol, Lieutenant Marco, is troubled by recurring nightmares of what happened in Manchuria and is put on sick-leave. He decides to visit Shaw and on the train meets Rosie (2) who comforts him during an attack of nerves. At Shaw's apartment, he is attacked by a Chinese agent (3) working as Shaw's houseboy but wins a gruelling Karate fight. He is arrested by the police and Rosie bails him out of jail.

Marco learns that another patrol member is suffering from the same nightmares. Marco's superiors now put him in charge of investigating Shaw. Still unaware that he is a tool of the 'Reds', Shaw marries an old girlfriend, Jocie, daughter of a liberal Senator, Thomas Jordon, after she appears dressed as the Queen of Diamonds at a fancy-dress ball (4).

Marco discovers that Shaw is triggered off by the Queen of Diamonds playing-card (5). Shaw's mother – the politically ambitious wife of a Red-baiting Senator, John Iselin – is the agent in control of her son (6) and she makes him kill Senator Jordan and Jocie.

Just before a big political rally, Marco attempts to persuade Shaw of what has happened to him (7). Shaw goes to a deserted spot in the convention hall with a high-powered rifle (8). He is to shoot the Presidential nominee and let Iselin into the White House. At the last moment, Shaw regains control of his actions and shoots his mother, Iselin (9) and himself.

1

2

3

4

5

6

7

8

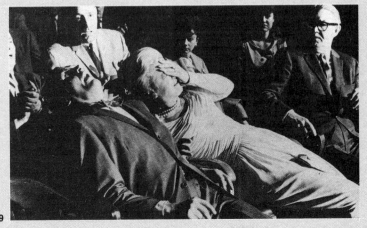

9

In the early Sixties the American cinema was obsessed with size – epic themes, wide screens, three-hour running times, all-star casts. Genre spectaculars – *The Guns of Navarone* (1961), *El Cid* (1961), *How the West Was Won* (1962) – lured audiences away from their TV sets in huge numbers.

The Great Escape is a typical product of this inflationary period, scarcely justifying its length, but zestfully directed by John Sturges. The script – a watered-down version of Paul Brickhill's largely factual account – is an anthology of genre clichés established in many British prisoner-of-war camp dramas of the Fifties, except that here there is a formidable American presence.

The British films, such as *The Wooden Horse* (1950) and *The Colditz Story* (1955), consciously strove to create a microcosm of England behind barbed wire, where attitudes of class could maintain morale and discipline. The deprivations and dangers of incarceration were minimized to strengthen the point about British resilience and the known outcome of the war; eccentricity and xenophobia became patriotic attributes, and quips like 'See you at Simpson's' served to promote a nostalgia that was fast fading.

The Germans were rarely cast as loathsome villains, but tended to be characterized as 'goons' – incompetent and obsequious. But as the Cold War developed, with Germany divided and suddenly the frontline of Allied defence, war films began to make distinctions between ordinary soldiers and officers who merely acted under orders, and the sadistic and fanatical SS men.

The Great Escape simply spreads this judicious blend of political diplomacy and Allied fervour on an unusually broad canvas, using an extensive and superbly designed set built on location in Bavaria. As with *The Guns of Navarone*, it is essentially an adventure drama, only incidentally a war film, with sharply defined characters played by charismatic stars.

Significantly, the film kills off the entire British contingent (Richard Attenborough, Donald Pleasence, Gordon Jackson, David McCallum) whilst the more resourceful and independently-minded Americans (the more expensive actors) survive. The massacre of Attenborough and his countrymen is shown and then forgotten in the closing images that pay tribute to Steve McQueen's star presence.

The film is in some ways a reworking of *The Magnificent Seven* (1960), having an equally memorable thematic score by Elmer Bernstein, and starring three of the 'seven': McQueen, Charles Bronson (playing a Pole) and James Coburn (playing an Australian). The fourth American is the amiable James Garner, and as a star vehicle the film is brilliantly organized.

Garner plays a versatile scrounger, Hendley – a humanized version of William Holden's Sefton in

The MIRISCH COMPANY Presents

Steve McQUEEN · James GARNER · Richard ATTENBOROUGH

A GLORIOUS SAGA OF THE R.A.F.

JOHN STURGES'

COLOUR BY DE LUXE
PANAVISION®

THE GREAT ESCAPE

JAMES **DONALD** · CHARLES **BRONSON** · DONALD **PLEASENCE** · JAMES **COBURN** · JOHN **LEYTON**

Produced & Directed by JOHN **STURGES** · Screenplay by JAMES **GLAVELL & BURNETT** · Based upon the book by PAUL **BRICKHILL**

Music by ELMER **BERNSTEIN** · A MIRISCH-ALPHA PICTURE · UNITED ARTISTS

Stalag 17 (1953). He puts his illicit 'general store' to good use, applying the Americanized hard-sell to a timid and stupid German called Werner who is terrified of being sent to the Russian front. Hendley's growing loyalty to the blind and feeble Blythe marks him as the American with heart – a soft-skinned cynic. Bronson's Danny Velinski represents bulging muscles and a neurotic mind – the conscience of the audience. James Coburn's Sedgwick is an irresistible image of stoicism whose outlandish suitcase upsets the bureaucratic British-run escape routine, but does not prevent his peaceful and picturesque jaunt on a stolen bicycle to neutral Switzerland.

But most noteworthy is Steve McQueen as Hilts, the quizzical, independent tough-guy who dominates the film, playing off superbly against Attenborough's stiff-upper-lip Squadron Leader Bartlett. Attenborough arrives at the camp preceded by his reputation as a fearless fighter and staunch ally, but it

is the expectations aroused by Hilts that generate most tension. *The Great Escape* strongly confirmed McQueen's stardom, and it ingeniously cheats its audience by regularly sending him into solitary confinement, away from the action. And yet McQueen's constant tossing of a baseball in his cell increases the tension within both

himself and the audience. When the escape finally comes, the film indulges McQueen's love of speed by granting him a cathartic motorcycle chase across open fields. His final crash into a barbed wire barrier – possibly a foretaste of the Iron Curtain – sensibly prevents him from turning into a comic strip hero.
ADRIAN TURNER

Directed by John Sturges, 1963
Prod co: Mirisch/Alpha. **prod:** John Sturges. **ass prod:** Robert E. Relyea. **sc:** James Clavell, W.R. Burnett, based on the book by Paul Brickhill. **photo** (De Luxe, Panavision): Daniel Fapp. **col:** De Luxe. **sp eff:** Paul Pollard. **ed:** Ferris Webster. **art dir:** Fernando Carrere. **cost:** Bert Henrikson. **mus:** Elmer Bernstein. **sd:** Harold Lewis. **ass dir:** Jack Reddish. **prod man:** Allen K. Wood. **r/t:** 173 minutes.
Cast: Steve McQueen (*Hilts*), James Garner (*Hendley*), Richard Attenborough (*Bartlett*), James Donald (*Ramsey*), Charles Bronson (*Danny Velinski*), Donald Pleasence (*Blythe*), James Coburn (*Sedgwick*), John Leyton (*Willie*), Gordon Jackson (*MacDonald*), David McCallum (*Ashley-Pitt*), Nigel Stock (*Cavendish*), William Russell (*Sorren*), Angus Lennie (*Ives*), Tom Adams (*Nimmo*), Robert Desmond (*Griffith*), Lawrence Montaigne (*Haynes*), Jud Taylor (*Goff*), Hannes Messemer (*Von Luger*), Robert Graf (*Werner*), Harry Riebauer (*Strachwitz*), Robert Freytag (*Posen*), Heinz Weiss (*Kramer*), Til Kiwe (*Frick*), Hans Reisser (*Kuhn*), George Mikell (*Dietrich*), Ulrich Beiger (*Preissen*), Karl Otto Alberty (*Steinbach*).

3

4

6

8

9

In 1942 Squadron Leader Bartlett arrives at Stalag Luft North, a top security German prisoner-of-war camp. He contacts Ramsay, the senior British officer, and proposes a mass breakout of 250 men. A nucleus of experts is assembled but an American –

Hilts – says he is breaking out next day (1). Testing a blind-spot between two watch-towers (2), Hilts is spotted and sent to the 'cooler' for solitary confinement, where he passes the time playing compulsively with a baseball.

Meanwhile, Bartlett's plan goes ahead and three tunnels – nicknamed Tom, Dick and Harry – are started. On his release Hilts volunteers to escape and be recaptured, after having memorized the surrounding countryside. Hilts has his day of freedom and is returned to the cooler. Another American, Hendley, scrounges special equipment from the Germans by bribing them with cigarettes and chocolate; Blythe forges identity papers; a Pole, Velinski, supervises the digging; others make civilian clothes and act as look-outs.

Hilts is released and starts an illicit distillery, and during impromptu Fourth of July

celebrations (3) the Germans discover Tom. Bartlett orders that all work be concentrated on Harry, and although Blythe begins to go blind, and Velinski suffers from claustrophobia (4), the tunnel is finally made ready. But because Harry is several yards short of the trees, the Germans discover the escape-in-progress (5) and only 76 men get away, travelling by train, plane, boat and on foot (6).

Hilts leads the Germans on a hair-raising motor-cycle chase, but crashes (7) and is arrested; Blythe is killed in a plane crash (8); Velinski and a few others manage to cross the border. Bartlett is recaptured after a chase in a village (9) and is summarily executed along with 50 others. As the Commandant leaves the camp in disgrace, some prisoners are returned – including Hendley and Hilts, the latter being thrown his baseball as he walks towards the cooler (10).

1

4

Clyde was the leader, Bonnie wrote poetry.

C.W. was a Myrna Loy fan who had a bluebird tattooed on his chest. Buck told corny jokes and carried a Kodak. Blanche was a preacher's daughter who kept her fingers in her ears during the gunfights. They played checkers and photographed each other incessantly. On Sunday nights they listened to Eddie Cantor on the radio. All in all, they killed 18 people.

They were the strangest damned gang you ever heard of.

WARREN BEATTY
FAYE DUNAWAY
BONNIE
AND CLYDE

MICHAEL J. POLLARD · GENE HACKMAN · ESTELLE PARSONS   DAVID NEWMAN and ROBERT BENTON Charles Strouse WARREN BEATTY ARTHUR PENN   TECHNICOLOR® A WARNER BROS.–SEVEN ARTS RELEASE W through Warner-Pathé

The original script of *Bonnie and Clyde* passed through divers hands before the finished film opened in America to critical indignation and audience acclaim. David Newman and Robert Benton first submitted their script to Jean-Luc Godard and then François Truffaut, both of whom suggested improvements before turning it down. Then Warren Beatty bought the property and persuaded Warner Brothers (the studio responsible for the great gangster movies of the Thirties) to finance it with Beatty as star and producer and Arthur Penn as director. Robert Towne, who later wrote *Chinatown* (1974) and Beatty's *Shampoo* (1975), polished the final draft without taking screen credit. The result was one of the most popular and influential films ever made in America.

It is intriguing to speculate what Godard and Truffaut might have made of such an essentially American subject. There are echoes of *Bande à Part* (1964, The Outsiders) and *Pierrot le Fou* (1965, Pierrot the Fool) in Penn's approach to genre and his abrupt changes of mood but the connection with the French *nouvelle vague* is more general than specific: like the early films of the *nouvelle vague*, *Bonnie and Clyde* liberated a national cinema from aesthetic stagnation and, in so doing, captured the imagination of American youth who regarded the values of Hollywood as anachronistic and its genres as moribund. Not since Nicholas Ray's *Rebel Without a Cause* (1955) had young Americans seen their frustrations articulated quite so forcefully on the screen.

The film's vivid account of social banditry paralleled the growing counter-culture and Vietnam protest movement and was developed in many subsequent films – *Alice's Restaurant*, *Easy Rider*, *Butch Cassidy and the Sundance Kid* (all 1969), *Bad Company* (1971), *Badlands* (1973). The commercial success of *Bonnie and Clyde* was merchandized in the form of nostalgia for Thirties music and fashion and inevitably led to a rash of gangster movies. The film's graphic violence ricocheted into the Seventies and Eighties.

If the film's style was refreshingly contemporary, the subject was far from new. *Persons in Hiding* (1939) and *The Bonnie Parker Story* (1958) attempted to portray the squalid facts of the case whilst *You Only Live Once* (1937), *They Live By Night* (1948) and *Gun Crazy* (1949) were adapted from the same source material. In fact, Bonnie Parker and Clyde Barrow scarcely rated more than a footnote in the history books and their robberies, punctuated by a dozen murders, were little more than petty thefts. Clyde was thought to have been homosexual and Bonnie's husband was a gang member but their legend as romantic fugitives grew from their instinct for publicity. Bonnie's doggerel verse and their snapshots were published in newspapers and earned them the status of folk-heroes to the destitute farmers of the southern states.

The real Bonnie and Clyde would have loved Penn's film because it is their pathetic image of themselves that is evoked so arrestingly. It is essentially a film about those most fundamental American impulses – celebrity and material and sexual success. The film's heroes are located within the mythology of cinema: Bonnie sees Ginger Rogers sing 'We're in the Money' from *Gold-Diggers of 1933* (1933); Clyde consciously models himself on Al Capone; the farmers they meet on the road resemble the Joads in *The Grapes of Wrath* (1940). Indeed, the Barrow gang move across the derelict landscape like movie stars, travelling players in a script which contrives for them a vanglorious death and posthumous fame.

Snapshots of the real gang – grainy and unglamorous – are behind the credits which fade to blood red. From here Penn cuts to the glamorous features of Beatty and Faye Dunaway. The other gang members are photographed throughout in unflattering light (and Buck and Blanche are later facially disfigured) but Bonnie and Clyde are always beautiful. This romantic idealism of them is ambiguous – the film remains sufficiently detached for the audience to identify with them and the visceral pleasure derived from their exploits. Their naivety and conceit is disarming and the film's jauntiness is both amusing and seductive. But gradually the viewer's pleasure is undercut by sudden irruptions of appalling violence – a Keystone Cops getaway turns sour when a bank clerk has his face blown off. The film becomes preoccupied with death, foretold by Bonnie's poem which releases Clyde's sexuality and hastens his end. The slow-motion massacre turns the heroes into frenzied corpses. The ugly and humourless Texas Ranger, Hamer, lowers his smoking carbine and stares directly into camera, in silent admonishment of our own impulses.

ADRIAN TURNER

7

Bonnie Parker is easily attracted by Clyde Barrow's reckless charm and when he nonchalantly robs a store she joins him (1) for a life of crime. After one of their hold-ups, they invite C. W. Moss, a car mechanic, to join them (2). The gang is completed by Buck, Clyde's ex-con brother, and his excitable wife, Blanche (3): they continue to rob banks.

The gang's exploits endear them to victims of the Depression but they narrowly avoid capture when the police surround their rented house (4, 5). Now wanted for murder, they are chased from state to state, notably by Sheriff Hamer who is humiliated when the trap he sets for them rebounds on himself.

2

3

5

6

9

8

Bonnie, though, senses the end is near and she visits her mother at a desolate rendezvous (6). Later the gang is ambushed (7), Buck is killed and Blanche, blinded, is taken prisoner. The others escape (8). C. W. takes Bonnie and Clyde to his father's house where they nurse their wounds (9). During this brief period of peace Bonnie has a poem published in a newspaper, and Clyde overcomes his impotence with Bonnie in a corn field.

Concerned for his son's safety, Mr Moss makes a deal with Hamer, and while driving in a quiet country lane (10 – production shot) Bonnie and Clyde die in a hail of bullets.

10

Directed by Arthur Penn, 1967
Prod co: Tatira/Hiller/Warner Bros. **prod:** Warren Beatty. **sc:** David Newman, Robert Benton. **photo** (Technicolor): Burnett Guffey. **ed:** Dede Allen. **art dir:** Dean Tavoularis, Raymond Paul. **mus:** Charles Strouse. **cost:** Theodora Van Runkle. **sd:** Francis E. Stahl. **r/t:** 111 minutes.
Cast: Warren Beatty (*Clyde Barrow*), Faye Dunaway (*Bonnie Parker*), Michael J. Pollard (*C. W. Moss*), Gene Hackman (*Buck Barrow*), Estelle Parsons (*Blanche*), Denver Pyle (*Frank Hamer*), Dub Taylor (*Ivan Moss*), Evans Evans (*Velma Davis*), Gene Wilder (*Eugene Grizzard*).

1

2

3

A brief introduction to *Butch Cassidy and the Sundance Kid* states: 'Not that it matters, but most of what follows is true'. The author was correct on both counts; the film *is* firmly based on the story of two outlaws at the turn of the century and it really does *not* matter that it is true, for it is one thing to base a script on real events and quite another to claim that the results are a 'true' representation of the facts.

The film is largely a vehicle for the Butch Cassidy (Paul Newman) and Sundance Kid (Robert Redford) relationship and the cinema has probably never produced a more endearing pair of villains. Butch is the thinker, a man who has vision 'and the rest of the world wears bifocals'. Sundance is the strong, more traditional type of Western hero who never uses two words when one will do. Together they rob banks and trains with such appealing politeness and ever-present incompetence that it is impossible not to like them.

For both actors it was an important film. Newman's previous major successes had been in roles where he was a rebellious loner – *The Hustler* (1961), *Hud* (1963), *Cool Hand Luke* (1967) – and his attempts at comedy are best forgotten.

6

Butch and Sundance, having extricated themselves from a card-game dispute (1), return to the Hole-in-the-Wall Gang's hideout (2) where Butch finds his leadership challenged by Harvey Logan (3). He re-establishes command but nevertheless accepts Harvey's idea of holding up the Union Pacific Flyer on successive runs.

After the first hold-up Sundance seeks out the attentions of teacher Etta Place and Butch demonstrates the wonders of a bicycle to the tune of 'Raindrops Keep Fallin' on My Head' (4).

The second Flyer hold-up is less accomplished than its predecessor; too much dynamite is used on the safe, and as the gang collects the scattered bank notes (5) another train appears. It contains a Superposse which had been formed with the specific purpose of eliminating the menace of Butch and Sundance.

Several members of the gang are shot down, but Butch and Sundance escape. However, the pursuit is relentless (6) and they become faced with the choice between a hopeless shoot-out or

7

8

4

5

Yet his screen relationship with Redford belied what had gone before; he gave a relaxed, amiable performance with a faintly sarcastic humour failing to mask a genuine affection for his partner.

But if the film was a well-received step in a new direction for Newman, it was a major milestone for Redford. *The Sundance Kid* quite simply made him one of the cinema's great names. The role drew attention to his good looks and even though the script offered him few words, the lines were good enough for him to prove that he was a competent actor.

Although the stars' performances were universally acclaimed and gave the film its identity, the Oscars went elsewhere: to William Goldman for his screenplay, Conrad Hall for cinematography, and Burt Bacharach for his musical score and – with lyricist Hal David – best song, 'Raindrops Keep Fallin' on My Head'. There were nominations for Best Picture and Best Direction but the film lost out to John Schlesinger's *Midnight Cowboy* (1969) in both instances.

However, the awards it received were a reflection that the film sought to entertain – it looked and sounded good. The ideas were not always startlingly original, with several echoing Arthur Penn's *Bonnie and Clyde* released two years earlier, but they were executed with style. For example, the sepia shots that open the film, depict the New York sojourn of Butch, Sundance and Etta (Katharine Ross), and provide the final image of the shoot-out, are strikingly effective. The middle sequence makes use of over three hundred stills in the space of a few minutes, an exciting piece of cinema that deserved to work.

It is ironic that William Goldman won his award for a screenplay which had an economy of words bordering on the miserly, but he relied on a terse, witty repartee between the two outlaws to create a feeling of jaunty optimism, combined with occasional moments of perceptive seriousness which hint at the inevitability of the final slaughter. 'Dammit, why is everything we're good at illegal?' they ask. 'Who are those guys?' they wonder in desperation as the law, in the shape of the Superposse, tries to catch up with them.

Their conversation has a casual, wry humour which at times is so anachronistic as to be absurd, but which works nevertheless. During the chase Butch asks Sundance 'I think we lost 'em. Do you think we lost 'em?' and when the reply is 'no' continues 'Neither do I'.

The lively banter carries on to the end when, surrounded by what looks like the greater part of the Bolivian army, they debate the possibility of emigrating to Australia. By then the opposition has mounted to impossible odds and their words have a pathos which the humour cannot hide.

Goldman has been taken to task for the lack of realism in his script and his interpretation of the story, for there is a great deal of evidence to suggest that Butch Cassidy survived and returned to the United States where he opened a business making adding machines.

However, the film that represents the West as it really was has probably yet to be made, as the cult of the Western has long since eclipsed the reality of its subject matter. The cinema presents a stylized, often romantic view of an era that provided – as with *Butch Cassidy and the Sundance Kid* – rich story pickings which could be embellished and transformed into entertainment. JOHN THOMPSON

Directed by George Roy Hill, 1969
Prod co: Campanile Productions/20th Century-Fox. A Newman-Foreman presentation. **prod:** John Foreman. **sc:** William Goldman. **photo** (Panavision, De Luxe Colour): Conrad Hall. **ed:** John C. Howard, Richard C. Meyer. **art dir:** Walter M. Scott, Chester L. Bayhi. **mus:** Burt Bacharach. **song:** 'Raindrops Keep Fallin' on My Head' by Burt Bacharach, Hal David, sung by B. J. Thomas. **r/t:** 110 minutes.
Cast: Paul Newman (*Butch Cassidy*), Robert Redford (*The Sundance Kid*), Katharine Ross (*Etta Place*), Strother Martin (*Percy Garris*), Henry Jones (*bicycle salesman*), Jeff Corey (*Sheriff Bledsoe*), George Furth (*Woodcock*), Cloris Leachman (*Agnes*), Ted Cassidy (*Harvey Logan*), Kenneth Mars (*marshal*), Donnelly Rodes (*Mason*), Jody Gilbert (*fat lady*), Timothy Scott (*'News' Carver*), Don Keefer (*fireman*), Charles Dierkop (*'Flat Nose' Curry*), Francisco Cordova (*bank manager*), Nelson Olmstead (*photographer*), Paul Bryar, Sam Elliott (*card players*), Charles Akins (*bank employee*), Eric Sinclair (*Tiffany salesman*), Dave Dunlap (*member of the gang*), Percy Helton (*old man*).

---

a near-suicidal leap from a clifftop. They leap (7).

Worried by their growing notoriety and the posse's professionalism, Butch, Sundance and Etta head for South America (8) after a short stay in New York. Bolivia's banks are the new target, but life again becomes dangerous as their reputation spreads from town to town.

Etta decides to return to the United States (9), leaving Butch and her lover to 'go straight' as payroll guards. However, they are robbed, and after retrieving the money return to outlaw status. While eating at an inn they are recognized and a detachment of the Bolivian army surrounds the town. Escape is finally made impossible (10).

9

10

THE WILD BUNCH

The Wild Bunch is bracketed by two extraordinary set-pieces of chaotically lethal action. The film begins with the frantic shoot-up – slaughtering sundry innocent bystanders – that ensues from the Bishop gang's aborted raid on the Starbuck bank; and ends with the orgiastic ritual of destruction in which – hugely outnumbered – the gang's ultimate survivors go down fighting as they manage to take a horde of Mapache's troops to perdition with them. Never before had carnage been so graphically or operatically wrought upon the screen.

It is probably these that are the sequences which pin down the film in the popular memory. For all that its protagonists – ageing gunfighters stranded by the rising tide of modern life – are men out of their time, Peckinpah's movie coincided spectacularly (in all senses) with a given moment in film history. Although Arthur Penn's Bonnie and Clyde (1967) two years earlier had pointed the way to a treatment of death and injury both franker and more elaborate than had previously been deemed acceptable, it was

The Wild Bunch that fully embraced this development. 'I wanted to show,' said Peckinpah, 'what the hell it feels like to get shot.'

In some of Peckinpah's subsequent films his preoccupation with savagery may become sterile or even absurd, and the slow-motion effects which – following Penn's example – he put to such striking use in The Wild Bunch would later, in his own and other hands, become a cliché. But here the explicitness of the scenes of carnage completely unites with the implications of the material: the members of the Wild Bunch can only achieve a kind of meaning for themselves in obliteration by violent death.

At one level, of course, the movie offers a repudiation of the chivalric trappings of the Western genre: Peckinpah extends the conventions of the anti-Westerns of a decade earlier, such as Delmer Daves' Cowboy (1958). Unlike the hired guns of The Magnificent Seven (1960), Bishop and his followers do not sign up on the side of the oppressed Mexican peasantry, but

rather with their corrupt oppressors. Indeed, the desperadoes who comprise the Bunch, ready to shoot down perfunctorily one of their own wounded when he is unable to keep up with them, would surely in an earlier vintage have been treated as antagonists rather than the 'heroes'.

Finally, though, and not simply through the force of Lucien Ballard's magisterial wide-screen images of horsemen traversing daunting landscapes and engaging in exploits of derring-do (such as the dynamite nonchalantly touched-off with a lighted cigar in the train robbery), the vision which the film asserts is a romantic one. The plot crucially turns on the mutual dependence of Bishop and Thornton (played with marvellously haggard strength by Robert Ryan), and the former clearly accepts that Thornton's dilemma in becoming the 'Judas goat' of the railroad bosses stems from Bishop's own

earlier lapse in allowing his old comrade to be captured.

There is, too, an almost luxuriant romanticism about the Mexican villagers' ceremonial farewell to Bishop and his men, a sequence which is repeated by Peckinpah at the film's very end. And eventually – though too late – the Bunch themselves set aside their façade of cynical pragmatism in abandoning Angel to his fate, and commit themselves to an heroically suicidal gesture on his behalf: 'This time,' declares Pike Bishop, 'let's do it right'.

The Wild Bunch is not without flaws: there is too apparent a recourse to literary metaphor in the deployment of children for ironic effect, and in such details as the vultures which symbolize the degenerate bounty hunters. But the defects fade to unimportance within the grandeur of the overall design. This is a movie of true size.

TIM PULLEINE

Directed by Sam Peckinpah, 1969
Prod co: Warner Brothers/Seven Arts. **prod:** Phil Feldman. **assoc. prod:** Roy N. Sickner. **prod man:** William Faralla. **2nd unit dir:** Buzz Henry. **sc:** Walon Green, Sam Peckinpah, from a story by Walon Green, Roy N. Sickner. **photo** (Technicolor, Panavision 70): Lucien Ballard. **ed:** Louis Lombardo. **art dir:** Edward Carrere. **mus:** Jerry Fielding. **sd:** Robert J. Miller. **ass dir:** Cliff Coleman, Fred Gamon. **r/t:** 145 minutes.
Cast: William Holden (Pike Bishop), Ernest Borgnine (Dutch), Robert Ryan (Deke Thornton), Edmond O'Brien (Sykes), Warren Oates (Lyle Gorch), Jaime Sanchez (Angel), Ben Johnson (Hector Gorch), Emilio Fernandez (Mapache), Strother Martin (Coffer), L. Q. Jones (T. C.), Albert Dekker (Harrigan), Bo Hopkins (Crazy Lee), Bud Taylor (Wainscoat), Jorge Russek (Zamorra), Alfonso Arau (Herrera), Chano Urueta (Don José), Sonia Amelio (Teresa), Aurora Clavel (Aurora), Elsa Cardenas (Elsa).

3

4

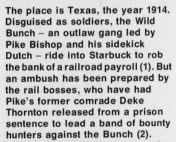

7

8

9

The place is Texas, the year 1914. Disguised as soldiers, the Wild Bunch – an outlaw gang led by Pike Bishop and his sidekick Dutch – ride into Starbuck to rob the bank of a railroad payroll (1). But an ambush has been prepared by the rail bosses, who have had Pike's former comrade Deke Thornton released from a prison sentence to lead a band of bounty hunters against the Bunch (2).

The ambush goes wrong, and in a hail of crossfire many of the townspeople are killed. Most of the gang escape, and after picking up their veteran comrade Sykes, deemed too old for action, they head into Mexico. There they encounter the villainous warlord 'General' Mapache (3), who hires them to steal guns from an American army munitions train. When Angel, a patriotic Mexican who rides with the Bunch, finds his girl is living with Mapache, a bloodbath is narrowly averted (4). After resting-up at Angel's home village, the gang goes ahead with the train robbery (5).

Bishop realizes that Thornton will be onto the scheme, but succeeds in outwitting him. Once the train has been held up, Mapache attempts to double-cross the Bunch in a canyon (6), but he is forestalled and has to pay up. However, Mapache finds out that Angel has given some of the stolen guns to Mexican revolutionaries, and takes him prisoner (7).

Initially, the Bunch abandon Angel to his fate, but after seeing

him tortured by Mapache, Pike, Dutch and the Gorch brothers (Sykes is left behind as look-out) enter Mapache's camp and demand Angel's release. In reply Mapache slits Angel's throat (8); Pike shoots Mapache dead (9), precipitating a bloody pitched battle between the Bunch and Mapache's troops, ending with no survivors (10). Later, Sykes appears on the scene with a group of revolutionaries; Thornton also arrives and decides to join them.

10

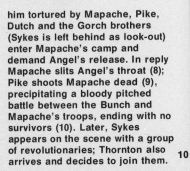

Detective Harry Callahan.
You don't assign him
to murder cases...

You just turn him loose.

Clint
Eastwood
Dirty Harry. x

CLINT EASTWOOD in "DIRTY HARRY" A Malpaso Company Production Co-Starring HARRY GUARDINO • RENI SANTONI • ANDY ROBINSON • JOHN LARCH and JOHN VERNON as "The Mayor" • Executive Producer Robert Daley • Screenplay by Harry Julian Fink & R. M. Fink and Dean Reisner • Story by Harry Julian Fink & R. M. Fink • Produced and Directed by Don Siegel • PANAVISION® • TECHNICOLOR® from Warner Bros., a Warner Communications company ⓌⒷ Released by Columbia-Warner Distributors Ltd.

Looking back over the Seventies, it is clear that the three most important movies in the commercial rise of the urban vigilante film were *Dirty Harry, Death Wish* (1974) and *The Exterminator* (1980). In the light of the two latter films it is now difficult to understand exactly why *Dirty Harry* caused all the stir and controversy it did when it first appeared. Its overt violence is minimal and what there is is hardly sadistic, at least not on the hero's part. Moreover, that hero is a policeman engaged in regular law-enforcement, rather than a private citizen carrying out a personal vendetta, and if his methods are rather unconventional and he chafes at the limitations imposed on him in his work by rules and regulations, at least the existence of these rules is acknowledged. In the end he throws away his police badge in a gesture of frustration but that can hardly be taken as an automatic sanction for everyone in the audience to go out after anyone who has somehow offended him.

All the same, in 1971 the film was freely accused of embodying a fascistic message and of endorsing Harry's most extreme digressions

1

2

3

5

6

from strict legality, thereby implying that the ends (the hunting down of an admitted psychopath) justified whatever means he might use. It is probable that *Dirty Harry* received such intense scrutiny because of its extreme efficacy as a piece of cinema entertainment: if Clint Eastwood is seen doing these things, supported by the film-making skills of Don Siegel, then the resulting effect on public morale might be expected to be that much more severe than if it was all happening in a lack-lustre programmer starring no-one in particular. And there was certainly no denying the overall class of the enterprise, any more than its logical place in the evolution of both Clint Eastwood's screen persona and the cinematic world of Don Siegel.

This was not the first film they had made together: it was preceded by *Coogan's Bluff* (1968), *Two Mules for Sister Sara* (1970) and *The Beguiled* (1971). Siegel also had a brief role in Eastwood's directorial debut *Play Misty for Me* (1971). After getting nowhere very much in Hollywood, Eastwood went to Europe and scored an enormous success in several 'spaghetti' Westerns direct-ed by Sergio Leone, starting with *Per un Pugno di Dollari* (1964, *A Fistful of Dollars*), in which he played a mysterious gunfighter with no apparent moral scruples and who used brutally ruthless tactics that were far from the cinema's time-honoured code of the West.

With *Coogan's Bluff* he made the vital transition from the West to the city: in it he plays a Western sheriff pursuing his man to New York and continuing to use the methods of the West, even though they mean exchanging horse for motor-bike and subsequently falling foul of his more bureaucratically-minded city colleagues.

Dirty Harry was a logical extension of this. Although Harry Callahan is San Francisco trained, he assumes an ignorance of city conventions which Coogan could naturally get away with, and evinces much of the ruthlessness that had made the Man With No Name of the Leone Westerns such a novelty; Harry flies in the face of police-thriller convention almost as much as his sinister predecessor does within the Western genre. There are a few attempts in the film to humanize and 'explain' him (by relaying how he lost his wife) but these seem to be mostly a matter of form and are not meant to be taken seriously. Essentially the character of Harry is given at the outset, derived more from the physical and emotional qualities of the star on screen than from any scriptwriter's dramaturgy.

On the whole, all explanation is kept to a minimum in *Dirty Harry*: the film's motivation is its action scenes. From the unsuccessful heist, stopped in its tracks almost single-handed by Harry early in the film, the tempo is created and kept up by the virtually wordless set-pieces that climax in Harry's running battle with the killer. This continuous momentum probably had more to do with the film's success than anything that might be construed as a 'message'. This, moviegoers felt, was the way they didn't make 'em any more: spare, hard-hitting muscular action such as is associated with the old-style macho-star vehicle.

It was no surprise that Eastwood went on to make two more films in which he played Harry Callahan: *Magnum Force* (1973) and *The Enforcer* (1976). It was also not too much of a surprise that in them he became more explicit about his mission, and that Siegel did not direct them. What had been fresh and spontaneous rapidly ran the risk of deteriorating into a formula, while as Eastwood became more established he tended to become more respectable. By 1976 a new star – also nurtured in Europe – emerged in Charles Bronson, and the genre had already moved on significantly with *Death Wish*. Nevertheless, *Dirty Harry* remains not only the first, but far and away the best of the bunch.

JOHN RUSSELL TAYLOR

Directed by Don Siegel, 1971
Prod co: Warner/Malpaso. **exec prod:** Robert Daley. **prod:** Don Siegel. **assoc prod:** Carl Pingatore. **sc:** Harry Julian Fink, Rita M. Fink, Dean Riesner. **photo** (Technicolor, Panavision): Bruce Surtees. **ed:** Carl Pingatore. **art dir:** Dale Hennessy. **set dec:** Robert DeVestel. **mus:** Lalo Schifrin. **sd:** William Randall. **ass dir:** Robert Rubin. **prod man:** Jim Henderling. **r/t:** 101 minutes.
Cast: Clint Eastwood (*Harry Callahan*), Harry Guardino (*Lt Bressler*), Reni Santoni (*Chico*), John Vernon (*the mayor*), Andy Robinson (*Scorpio*), John Larch (*Chief*), John Mitchum (*De Georgio*), Mae Mercer (*Mrs Russell*), Lyn Edgington (*Norma*), Ruth Kobart (*bus driver*), Woodrow Parfrey (*Mr Jaffe*), Josef Sommer (*Rothko*), William Patterson (*Bannerman*), James Nolan (*liquor proprietor*), Maurice S. Argent (*Sid Kleinman*), Jo de Winter (*Miss Willis*), Craig G. Kelly (*Sgt Reineke*).

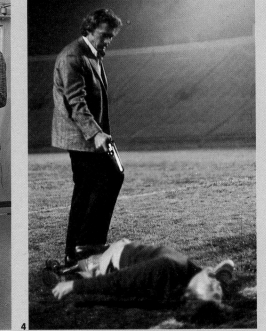

4

Inspector Harry Callahan of the San Francisco police force, known as Dirty Harry because of his ruthless methods (1) and tendency to accept unpleasant assignments, is given the job of capturing Scorpio, a rooftop sniper (2) who is attempting to hold the city to ransom. Scorpio kills twice to prove he means business, then kidnaps a girl.

Against his will, Harry finds himself with Chico, a new partner fresh from college (3). However, when Harry delivers the ransom money for the girl's release he is nearly killed and it is only Chico's intervention that saves him.

Chasing the wounded Scorpio to a football stadium, Harry manages to force him to reveal the girl's whereabouts before turning him in (4). The girl proves to be dead but Harry's use of strong-arm tactics while extracting the information enables the killer to be released on a legal technicality.

A disillusioned Chico leaves the force but Harry takes the law into his own hands and continues to pursue Scorpio, who retaliates by arranging for himself to be beaten up (5) in an attempt to frame Harry for assault. After this fails, Scorpio then kidnaps a bus-load of school-children.

Against orders, Harry rescues the children. Scorpio flees the bus (6), but Harry finally tracks him down (7) and 'executes' him (8). As he turns to walk away, Harry hurls his police badge into the river.

Shaft spearheaded the wave of blaxploitation pictures that flooded the screens in the early Seventies. The Hollywood image of the black had been liberalized in the Fifties and Sixties by the ebony-saint figures of Poitier and Belafonte, thereby displacing the patronizing sambo stereotype. By the Seventies, movies showed that a black could be as rough, tough, wise-cracking and heroic as any white gumshoe. The parallels were explicitly drawn in the advertising for *Shaft*, 'Hotter than Bond, Cooler than Bullitt'.

Shaft was not the first film with a black hero: Poitier played a police detective in Norman Jewison's Oscar winner *In the Heat of the Night* (1967); and Jim Brown — an ex-football professional — played a succession of action heroes, most notably in *Rio Conchos* (1964), *The Dirty Dozen* (1967), *The Split* (1968), *100 Rifles* (1969), *Tick . . . Tick . . . Tick*, *The Grasshopper* and *El Condor* (all 1970).

However, these forerunners varied significantly from *Shaft*. While the Poitier movies focused on racial themes, *Shaft* relegated racial questions to the taken-for-granted background. It is true that the reward money given to the black militants who help Shaft is donated to a fund for political prisoners, but *Shaft* is no message movie. The director, Gordon Parks, disclaimed any political intent — 'It's just a Saturday night fun picture which people go to see because they want to see the black guy winning' — although he did stress that the very fact of having a black hero was significant.

Shaft also departed from the Jim Brown films in that most of the protagonists were black and the action was largely set in Harlem. In Brown's movies he frequently had white co-stars; although when Brown made love on screen — as in his much publicized bedroom scenes with Raquel Welch in *100 Rifles* — the script meekly hedged the miscegenation issue by making the woman a half-caste. *Shaft* fully exploits the prowess, sexual and violent, suggested by his name — 'Shaft's his name. Shaft's his game', the posters proclaimed. Shaft has a black mistress but frequently picks up white women and takes them back to his luxurious Greenwich Village pad. To the James Bond swinging man-of-action style, Shaft adds the mystique of black hyper-virility and, when asked by a young policeman where he is going, Shaft replies, 'I'm going to get laid. Where are you going?'

The film that paved the way for *Shaft* was *Cotton Comes to Harlem* (1970). This was derived from Chester Himes' detective books about two Harlem cops, and whereas Sidney Poitier's portrayal of Virgil Tibbs had been largely aimed at white audiences, *Cotton Comes to Harlem* was pitched directly at the heart of the ghetto audience by its black director Ossie Davis. The film was a huge hit and it was estimated that over 70 per cent of its audience was black, a sure pointer to the lucrative, hitherto untapped potential of the black market.

The result was the blaxploitation cycle of the early Seventies, in which white producers financed black directors to put black performers through all the action paces of the conventional thriller — often directly remaking white successes as in *Black Gunn*, *Cool Breeze* (both 1972), and *Black Caesar* (1973), *Cool Breeze* being derived from *The Asphalt Jungle* (1950). The cycle's death knell was sounded by various bizarre attempts to blend it with other current fashions, notably the mid-Seventies blaxploitation meets Kung Fu films such as *Black Belt Jones* (1974).

The high point of the cycle was without doubt *Shaft*, the only entry achieving any significant crossover success with white audiences. It effectively combined all the ingredients of the popular white thriller with black appeal. A taut, fast-moving pace was provided by Gordon Parks who had just the right background for the assignment; the last of 15 children from a poor black Kansas farm family, he had played piano in a Minnesota bordello, and been a Harlem dope-runner and professional basketball player before achieving success as a photographer and reporter for *Life* magazine. Richard Roundtree, a former college football star and male model, had the right blend of sophistication, sexuality and toughness for the Shaft character.

Shaft's script, peppered with Chandleresque wisecracks and ghetto humour, was provided by Ernest Tidyman, author of the original novel and writer of the similarly successful *The French Connection* (1971). The screenplay explicitly draws a parallel between *Shaft* and

Hotter than Bond,
Cooler than Bullitt.

SHAFT's his name.
SHAFT's his game.

METRO-GOLDWYN-MAYER Presents "SHAFT" Starring RICHARD ROUNDTREE · Co-Starring MOSES GUNN · Screenplay by ERNEST TIDYMAN and JOHN D. F. BLACK · Based upon the novel by ERNEST TIDYMAN · Music by ISAAC HAYES · Produced by JOEL FREEMAN · Directed by GORDON PARKS METROCOLOR · Released by MGM-EMI

Directed by Gordon Parks, 1971
Prod co: MGM/Shaft Productions. A Stirling Silliphant/Roger Lewis Production. **prod:** Joel Freeman. **assoc prod:** David Golden. **sc:** Ernest Tidyman, John D. F. Black, from the novel by Ernest Tidyman. **photo** (Metrocolor): Urs Furrer. **ed:** Hugh A. Robertson. **art dir:** Emanuel Gerard. **mus:** Isaac Hayes. **sd:** Lee Bost, Hal Watkins. **ass dir:** Ted Zachary. **prod man:** Steven Skloot. **r/t:** 100 minutes.
Cast: Richard Roundtree (*John Shaft*), Moses Gunn (*Bumpy Jonas*), Charles Cioffi (*Vic Androzzi*), Christopher St John (*Ben Buford*), Gwenn Mitchell (*Ellie Moore*), Lawrence Pressman (*Tom Hannon*), Victor Arnold (*Charlie*), Sherri Brewer (*Marcy*), Rex Robbins (*Rollie*), Camille Yarbrough (*Dina Green*), Margaret Warncke (*Linda*), Joseph Leon (*Byron Leibowitz*), Arnold Johnson (*Cul*), Dominic Barto (*Patsy*), George Strus (*Carmen*), Edmund Hashim (*Lee*), Drew Bundini Brown (*Willy*), Tommy Lane (*Leroy*), Al Kirk (*Sims*), Shimen Ruskin (*Dr Sam*), Antonio Fargas (*Bunky*), Gertrude Jeanette (*old lady*), Lee Steele (*blind vendor*), Damu King (*Mal*), Donny Burks (*Remmy*), Tony King (*Davies*), Benjamin Rixon (*Bey Newfield*), Ricardo Brown (*Tully*), Alan Weeks (*Gus*), Glen Johnson (*Char*), Dennis Tate (*Dotts*), Adam Wade, James Hainesworth (*brothers*), Clee Burtonia (*Sonny*), Ed Bernard (*Peerce*), Ed Barth (*Tony*), Joe Pronto (*Dom*), Robin Nolan (*waitress*), Ron Tannas (*Billy*), Betty Bresler (*Mrs Androzzi*), Gonzalo Madurga (*counterman*), Paul Nevens (*elevator man*), Jon Richards (*elevator starter*).

the earlier traditions of *film noir* when the hero is described as a 'black Sam Spade'. Another vital contributor to *Shaft*'s success was the pulsating theme music by Isaac Hayes, the Oscar-winning song for that year.

This potent brew of black 'Bondage' was an enormous hit. MGM rushed into producing a sequel, *Shaft's Big Score!* (1972), which despite the same star, director, writer, musical style and larger budget, failed to match the success of the original. By the time the final entry in the trilogy appeared in 1973, the blaxploitation cycle had run its course. Despite the interesting idea of having Shaft seek out his roots and fight the slave trade, *Shaft in Africa* (this time scripted by Stirling Silliphant and directed by John Guillermin) bombed at the box-office. Seeing the writing on the wall, MGM sold the Shaft property to television, but the show barely lasted a season.

Critical response to *Shaft* was bitterly divided. White and black liberals decried the new superstud, superhero image of the black man, and the film's emphasis on Playboy-style consumption, as being but a new and derogatory racist stereotype. The film's supporters pointed to its immense popularity amongst blacks, and recognized the expression of ghetto audience's bitterness and hostility. It was also stressed that *Shaft*'s success paved the way for more black performers, directors and technicians in Hollywood — although this effect has been ephemeral.

However, the demonstration that a black super-hero could be big box-office remains a significant milestone in Hollywood's portrayal of the blacks.   ROBERT REINER

54

Black private-eye John Shaft is tipped off that two black hoods want to see him. He finds them waiting for him in his Times Square office (1), and after disposing of one of them by throwing him out of the window, he makes the other admit that Bumpy Jonas – a Harlem underworld boss – sent them.

Police Lieutenant Vic Androzzi (2) 'persuades' Shaft – by threatening to take away his licence – to help him investigate Jonas' operations. Jonas then visits Shaft in person (3) and asks him to find his daughter Marcy whom he believes has been kidnapped by Ben Buford, a black militant and old friend of Shaft. After tracing Ben to an uptown tenement (4), they are attacked by unknown gunmen and forced to flee. Shaft convinces Ben that he did not engineer the ambush and they confront Jonas, accusing him of the raid (5). Jonas denies it but admits that he wanted to locate Ben and his militants to seek their help.

Jonas and the police receive confirmation that Marcy has been kidnapped by the Mafia who aim to take over the Harlem rackets. Shaft locates them and tries to make a deal (6), but is shot in the process. He and Ben follow Marcy and her captors to an uptown hotel and as Ben's men cover him (7) Shaft crashes into her room and rushes her to safety (8). Shaft then calls up Lieutenant Androzzi and tells him the case is his to wrap up.

In 1972 Paramount decided to make *The Godfather* the centrepiece of their new production strategy. The aim was to find one film a year that would be a really big box-office success, a success large enough to carry all the other productions. The right film would have the benefit of both a large production and promotions budget, and it would be exhibited in such a way as to gain maximum impact – simultaneous, nationwide release backed by intense publicity. This impact would then be exploited by charging higher admission prices.

The choice of *The Godfather* proved inspired. The film was an extravagant commercial success. Within days of its release it had recovered all initial outlay, and within weeks had become an extremely profitable enterprise. In commercial terms *The Godfather* became a landmark, an indication of what could be achieved by Paramount's scheme. It was also a landmark in less tangible ways. The director, Francis Ford Coppola, was seen as a representative of the new generation of Hollywood filmmakers, and the success of the film guaranteed not only his artistic future but also improved the prospects of his contemporaries.

Although it was directed by a 'new' film-maker, *The Godfather* is essentially a traditional film: the subject-matter – the world of ethnic crime – is familiar and has provided the basis for many previous films; the main thrust is a narrative one, though ranging widely in time and space; the story is told vividly and clearly; the stars are a mixture of established faces, such as Marlon Brando and Sterling Hayden, and promising newcomers – Al Pacino, James Caan and Diane Keaton.

In many ways what separates *The Godfather* from previous gangster films is the amount of money spent on it. This is not as cynical a comment as it sounds, for the money is translated into artistic values on the screen. It allows the narrative to develop in a leisurely way, giving the actors the opportunity to develop characterizations and allowing settings and costumes to have strong dramatic presence. Overall, the money enables the film to be turned into a substantial spectacle.

Of course, the availability of money does not guarantee its effective use; it is up to the film-maker to take advantage of the resources money brings within reach. Coppola's contribution to *The Godfather* is undoubtedly a crucial one. As a director, his talents incline towards the creation of spectacle, and like a director of musicals, he is able to choreograph the movement of large numbers of people; the opening wedding reception is a superb example in this respect. He is always conscious of the expressive use of colour; the contrast between the light golden tones of the Sicilian sequences and the dark, sombre ones of the interiors inhabited by the gangsters is striking. Coppola also seems particularly sensitive to the emotional physical presence of actors and actresses.

PARAMOUNT PICTURES PRESENTS

The Godfather

The Godfather is finely cast – Brando's considered authority, Al Pacino's controlled intensity, Robert Duvall's distanced influence, Diane Keaton's directness and vulnerability.

It has been said that *The Godfather* is a radical film. This is a difficult argument to sustain, for the points the film makes about the place of crime in American society (its intimate connections with the established representatives of law and politics, its control over legitimate enterprises, the analogies that can be made between the way crime and large corporations conduct their affairs) are all familiar ones, and hardly the marks of a radical view of American society. If anything, the film, with its admiration for a certain ideal of masculine purity based on honour, ruthlessness, the use of violence and the maintenance of the family, is reactionary in outlook.

The popular success of *The Godfather* is not easy to explain. The film's overall effect is rather cold and bleak and the ruthlessness of the central characters, their commitment to violence and repression of emotion make identification hard. A fictional world without moral basis, and characterized by bloody struggles, is not immediately attractive. However, some of the film's appeal can be explained. It has many of the pleasures of the nineteenth-century realist novel, providing an alternative social world that the reader or viewer can inhabit; it has a sense of the epic in its presentation of warring kingdoms whose rise and fall effect the lives of ordinary people, not just those of the chieftains.

But whatever *The Godfather*'s appeal, it certainly doesn't sustain the view of many film producers and critics that the popular audience is looking for easy identifications and comfortable reassurances. The popular response is far more complicated that that.

ALAN LOVELL

Don Vito Corleone (1) – head of an Italian-American criminal 'family' and 'Godfather' to the Italian immigrants in New York – holds a lavish reception for his daughter's wedding (2), periodically returning to his office to settle any 'business' that crops up during the day.

The Don's power is illustrated when Johnny Fontane, a singing star he has backed (3), seeks his help in getting a part in a Hollywood movie. The Don asks the producer, Jack Woltz, to give Fontane the part. When friendly persuasion fails, Woltz finds the severed head of his favourite horse in bed with him. Fontane is given the part.

Another family, the Tattaglias, propose that the Don join in their drug-running trade. When he refuses, the Tattaglias shoot him down in the street (4). The Don survives, but his younger son Michael (5) takes revenge by killing a Tattaglia associate (6). He flees to Sicily (7) where he settles down and marries a local girl.

After two years news of his brother Sonny's death reaches Michael. His wife is then killed by a car bomb meant for him (8) and he returns to America. When the Don dies of a heart attack Michael becomes the leader of the 'family'.

A series of ruthless measures finally reinstates the Corleone family's position. A new Godfather has emerged in his father's image (9).

Directed by Francis Ford Coppola, 1972
Prod co: Alfran Productions. **prod:** Albert S. Ruddy. **assoc prod:** Gray Frederickson. **sc:** Mario Puzo, Francis Ford Coppola, from the novel by Mario Puzo. **photo** (Technicolor): Gordon Willis. **sp eff:** A. D. Flowers, Jow Lombardi, Sass Bedig. **ed:** William Reynolds, Peter Zinner, Marc Laub, Murray Solomon. **art dir:** Warren Clymer, Philip Smith. **cost:** Anna Hill Johnstone. **mus:** Nino Rota. **mus dir:** Carlo Savina. **sd:** Christopher Newman, Les Lazarowitz, Bud Grenzbach, Richard Portman. **ass dir:** Fred Gallo, Tony Brandt. **prod man:** Fred Caruso, Valerio De Paolis. **r/t:** 175 minutes.
Cast: Marlon Brando (*Don Vito Corleone*), Al Pacino (*Michael Corleone*), James Caan (*Sonny Corleone*), Richard Castellano (*Clemenza*), Robert Duvall (*Tom Hagen*), Sterling Hayden (*McCluskey*), John Marley (*Jack Woltz*), Richard Conte (*Barzini*), Diane Keaton (*Kay Adams*), Al Lettieri (*Sollozzo*), Abe Vigoda (*Tessio*), Talia Shire (*Connie Rizzi*), Gianni Russo (*Carlo Rizzi*), John Cazale (*Fredo Corleone*), Rudy Bond (*Cuneo*), Al Martino (*Johnny Fontane*), Morgana King (*Mama Corleone*), Lenny Montana (*Luca Brasi*), John Martino (*Paulie Gatto*), Salvatore Corsitto (*Bonasera*), Richard Bright (*Neri*), Alex Rocco (*Moe Greene*), Tony Giorgio (*Bruno Tattaglia*), Vito Scotti (*Nazorine*), Tere Livrano (*Theresa Hagen*), Victor Rendina (*Phillip Tattaglia*), Jeannie Linero (*Lucy Mancini*), Julie Gregg (*Sandra Corleone*), Ardell Sheridan (*Mrs Clemenza*), Simonetta Stefanelli (*Apollonia*), Angelo Infanti (*Fabrizio*), Corrado Gaipa (*Don Tommasino*), Franco Citti (*Calo*), Saro Urzi (*Vitelli*).

MEAN

1

STREETS

The opening credits of *Mean Streets* – a haphazard sequence of hand-held home-movie shots backed by the punchy music of the Ronettes singing 'Be My Baby' – end on a shot of Charlie, the small-time gangster, shaking hands with the parish priest. Both men are smiling at the camera. Over this image the final title reads 'directed by Martin Scorsese'. It is a shot that

encapsulates the two career choices Scorsese reckons were offered to him by his upbringing in New York's Little Italy district.

He had already failed to stay the course in a Catholic seminary, and his slight stature and asthmatic condition did not mark him out as a future Lucky Luciano, though the hit-man fantasy is fulfilled briefly at the end of *Mean Streets* when the

director himself plays the killer hired to exact revenge on Johnny Boy. For the rest of the movie, however, the feeling that Scorsese is living *through* the character of Charlie is inescapable, and the persona had already been sketched in by Harvey Keitel in Scorsese's earlier movie *Who's That Knocking at My Door?* (1968).

The key to the critical and commercial success of *Mean Streets* lies in the circumstances of its financing and in Scorsese's own background: the common denominator is rock music. Determined to make the film he had been planning in his head for years and resisting the temptation to film another Roger Corman quickie after *Boxcar Bertha* (1972), Scorsese found a backer in Jonathan Taplin, who managed bookings and tours for Bob Dylan and The Band.

From the start Scorsese had conceived the film in terms of its picture track and its music track simultaneously. His own experience as an editor on several rock-concert movies in the early Seventies testified to his professional knowledge of the music business. But above all it was Scorsese's memory of Sixties rock'n'roll with its revolutionary power to influence people's lives and behaviour that made *Mean Streets* such an exciting proposition for Taplin and Warner Brothers.

In the film, music is always of equal importance to the other elements of *mise-en-scène* – lighting, positioning of actors, movement of

camera, and so on. The fight in Joey's pool-room, for example, lasts exactly the length of the Marvelettes' number 'Please Mr Postman' and the action – filmed in a combination of threatening close-ups, giddy overhead shots and rapid, hand-held takes pursuing the brawlers around the room – is cut neatly to the rhythm of the song. For once, the epithet 'operatic' is entirely appropriate, especially given Scorsese's use of Italian popular classics and the cultural importance of opera within the Italian immigrant society depicted in the film.

But *Mean Streets* also distances Scorsese from his background; ironically, the film was shot not in the New York streets where it is set but in Los Angeles. More importantly, it reveals the gap between Scorsese the film-maker and those adolescent options of priest or gangster. It is a distance that is measured in the film by quotations from other movies. When Michael and Charlie go to a cinema on the proceeds of a con-trick, the film they see is John Ford's *The Searchers* (1956) and Scorsese shows a clip with John Wayne in a brawl. But when Charlie and Johnny Boy go on the run from Michael, the cinema they shelter in is showing a horror movie with Vincent Price about to be consumed in the flames of hell.

Earlier, when Charlie and Teresa make love in a hotel room, Scorsese quotes quite consciously from the director Jean-Luc Godard – Harvey Keitel and Amy Robinson replay the Jean-Paul Belmondo and Jean Seberg roles from *A Bout de Souffle* (1960, *Breathless*). The director even ventures a jump-cut, more as an acknowledgment of Godard's influence than as a device within the narrative.

All the examples of cine-literacy (referring, within one film, to a whole context of cinematic influences, both European and American) are characteristic of the 'movie brat' generation of film-makers. In *Mean Streets* they are brilliantly combined with superb ensemble, improvisatory acting from Keitel, De Niro and Romanus, to produce a work that is, if anything, even more exciting on a formal level than in its gripping, breathless narrative.

MARTYN AUTY

Directed by Martin Scorsese, 1973
Prod co: Taplin-Perry-Scorsese for Warner Brothers. **exec prod:** E. Lee Perry. **prod:** Jonathan T. Taplin. **sc:** Martin Scorsese, Mardik Martin, from a story by Martin Scorsese. **photo** (Technicolor): Kent Wakeford. **add photo:** Norman Gerard. **visual consultant:** David Nichols. **sp eff:** Bill Bales. **ed:** Sid Levin. **songs:** 'Jumping Jack Flash', 'Tell Me' by The Rolling Stones, 'I Love You So' by The Chantells, 'Addio Sogni Di Gloria', 'Conta per' Me', 'Manasterio Di Santa Chiara' by Giuseppe De Stefano, 'Marruzella', 'Scapricciatiello' by Renato Carosone, 'Please Mr Postman' by The Marvelettes, 'Hideaway', 'I Looked Away' by Eric Clapton, 'Desiree' by The Chants, 'Rubber Bisquit' by The Chips, 'Pledging My Love' by Johnny Ace, 'Ritino Sabroso' by Ray Baretta, 'You' by The Aquatones, 'Ship of Love' by The Nutmegs, 'Florence' by The Paragons, 'Malafemmina' by Jimmy Roselli, 'Those Oldies But Goodies' by Little Caesar and the Romans, 'I Met Him on a Sunday' by The Shirelles, 'Be My Baby' by The Ronettes, 'Mickey's Monkey' by The Miracles. **sd:** Glen Glenn. **sd rec:** Don Johnson, John K. Williamson, Bud Grenzbach, Walter Goss. **stunts co-ordinator:** Bill Katching. **animal trainer:** George Toth. **prod man:** Paul Rapp. **ass dir:** Russell Vreeland, Ron Satloff. **r/t:** 110 minutes.
Cast: Harvey Keitel (*Charlie*), Robert De Niro (*Johnny Boy*), David Proval (*Tony*), Amy Robinson (*Teresa*), Richard Romanus (*Michael*), Cesare Danova (*Giovanni*), Victor Argo (*Mario*), Robert Carradine (*assassin*), Jeannie Bell (*Diane*), D'Mitch Davis (*cop*), David Carradine (*drunk*), George Memmoli (*Joey*), Murray Mosten (*Oscar*), Ken Sinclair (*Sammy*), Harry Northup (*soldier*), Lois Walden (*Jewish girl*), Lenny Scarletta (*Jimmy*), Robert Wilder (*Benton*), Martin Scorsese (*car gunman*), Dino Seragusa (*old man*), Peter Fain (*George*), Julie Andelman (*girl at party*), Jaime Alba, Ken Konstantin (*young boys*), Nicki 'Ack' Aqualino (*man on docks*), B. Mitchell Reed (*disc jockey*), Catherine Scorsese (*neighbour on staircase*).

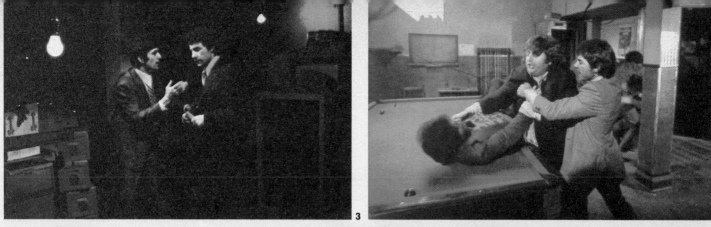

2

3

4

5

Home-movie footage introduces the principal characters – Charlie, Johnny Boy and Michael – in their neighbourhood of Little Italy, New York. Charlie (1), a practising but spiritually anguished Catholic, works as a collector for his mafioso uncle, Giovanni. Michael, a small-time crook, has loaned money to the irresponsible Johnny Boy who cannot hold down a job long enough to make regular repayments to him.

Charlie stands surety for Johnny Boy, but in the back-room of Tony's club (2) he berates him for his irresponsible attitude.

Later, Charlie, Johnny Boy, Tony and another associate, Jimmy, call at Joey's pool-room to make a collection. A fight breaks out over an insult (3) but just as all is settled between the two sides, Johnny Boy throws a final punch and is bundled out.

Meanwhile, Charlie is dating

Johnny Boy's cousin Teresa (4), despite a warning from uncle Giovanni not to associate with the family at all (5).

When Johnny Boy shows up over an hour late at Teresa's, Charlie attacks him (6) and then drags him off to Tony's, where they have a crucial meeting with Michael. At Tony's, Michael demands his repayment from Johnny Boy, who offers him ten dollars, insults him and then pulls

a gun on him (7). Michael walks out in a rage.

Charlie hustles Johnny Boy out of the club, knowing that Michael will come looking for revenge. As Charlie, Johnny Boy and Teresa are driving out of town, Michael's car pulls alongside and a hired gunman fires several shots, hitting Johnny Boy in the neck (8) and wounding the other two. Charlie staggers from the crashed car and slumps to his knees (9).

6

7

8

9

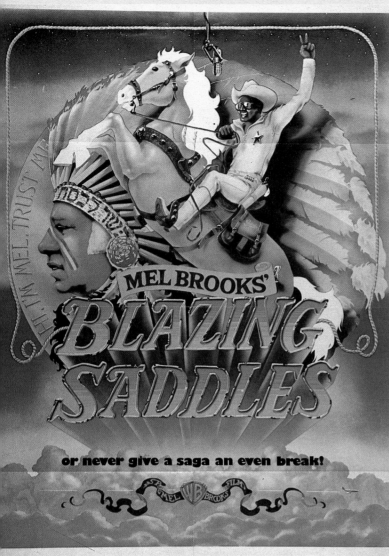

1

4

7

Mel Brooks' *Blazing Saddles* is unique among black exploitation films of the Sixties and Seventies – it refuses to take *anything* about colour seriously, and it refuses to exploit. Cleverly disguised as a send-up of a Hollywood Western, it uses satire and shocking bad taste to lampoon the guilt-inspired new white liberal racial attitudes of the time, while gleefully poking large, rude holes in the new black stereotypes Hollywood invented to cash in on them.

An unredeemed iconoclast, Mel Brooks loves to burlesque showbiz subjects in his films. *Blazing Saddles*, his Hollywood blast, is by far and away the most disrespectful, but as plain parody, it is not particularly successful. Hilarious in places, sometimes brilliant, it is nevertheless too undisciplined and excessive in its ridicule to match subtler, better-structured Western spoofs like *Destry Rides Again* (1939) or *Cat Ballou* (1965).

The racial material works well, however. *Blazing Saddles* is perhaps the only black film by a white film-maker that actually says some-

thing useful about the black-white dilemma as popular mythology. Its subversive balloon-puncturing warns against becoming too comfortable with Hollywood's celluloid vision of the race situation and its convenient synthesizing of black characters to function within it. (No black man is really like Shaft or Virgil Tibbs, just as no black man was ever like Uncle Tom.) What Brooks aims to do is remind the gullible that Hollywood will co-opt any potentially profitable social issue – drug addiction, prostitution, organized crime, juvenile delinquency, and race – and distort it for consumption's sake in the direction of over-simplification and plausibility. Brooks is a good radical humanist. He doesn't like the way Hollywood lulls its audiences. He wants to shock people into awareness and dispel complacency.

From the opening seconds, when the Warner Brothers logo disintegrates in flames, Brooks announces exactly what *Blazing Saddles* is about: Hot Air. The title, reduced to its initials, underlines the point. And the joke is driven home when

the cowboys' wind-breaking spree around the camp-fire after a meal of beans clicks with the line in Frankie Laine's title song which calls the hero's blazing saddle a beacon of justice. Once set up, the lavatorial humour continues non-stop: a barrage of unimaginably crude jokes about 'niggers' that are designed to make white liberal audiences wince with embarrassment. Most of the gags work beautifully: as when the harassed Negro sheriff, Black Bart, forced into confrontation with the hostile townsfolk, fast-draws his six-shooter and then aims it at his own head; or when the black road gang, ordered by the rednecks to sing a good ol' nigger work-song, go into a crooning, MGM rendition of 'I Get a Kick Out of You' – only to

be topped by the bigots in a rousing, minstrel-show version of 'De Camptown Races' (heavy on the 'camp'). In one glorious white-baiting moment, Black Bart reaches deep into the front of his jeans and says, 'Excuse me while I whip this out' – and produces a legal document. Lili Von Shtupp, the honky-tonk seductress hired to undo the black sheriff, continues this gag when – finally seduced herself by the myth of black sexual prowess into joining the good guys – she invites Bart into her darkened hotel room and murmurs, 'Is it true you people are so, mm, gifted?', only to hear Bart lisp, 'Yeth, it's twoo . . . it's *twoo*'.

As in all of Brooks' films, there is a weakness for breaking context

The baffled, incompetent Black Bart – rescued from servitude on a railroad gang, from drowning in quicksand (1), and from hanging for hitting his white foreman with a shovel – is suddenly taken up by the crooked lawyer Hedley Lamarr and the corrupt, windbag Governor William J. Lepetomane (2). To his horror he is made sheriff of Rock Ridge, a miserable, all-white cow-town that Lamarr and Lepetomane hope to rip off in a land swindle.

Bart gets a glacial welcome from the townsfolk (3) but finds an ally in the boozed, redemption-seeking Waco Kid (4), one-time fast-draw legend. With Waco's help, Bart discovers he isn't as useless as everyone thought, a discovery that infuriates the villains and leads them to send Lili Von Shtupp (5), irresistible

blonde seductress, to destroy the ungrateful nigger so they can get on with their devious schemes. But Bart wins Lili's affections, leaving the baddies no choice but to hire a gang of desperadoes to wreck the town and kill Bart.

A brilliant plan is needed and Bart, aided by Waco (6), comes up with it at the last moment: a substitute cardboard town and a lot of dynamite win the day, save the real town, and enshrine Bart as the all-time hero of Rock Ridge. The big fight at the end bursts its sound-stage bounds (7) and spills over into the streets of 'real' Hollywood (8 – production shot). The two heroes, Bart and Waco, ride their horses into Grauman's Chinese Theatre to watch the happy ending of their own movie, then ride off into the sunset in a limousine.

too violently in order to pull a far-out gag that hardly belongs – the sudden discovery of Count Basie's band playing the film score in the middle of the desert, for example, and the recruiting of gunslingers from an improbable Central Casting gang of Arabs, Hell's Angels and hooded Klansmen. Such moments make Brooks look either out of control or not as committed to his objective as he ought to be. They are also the moments that ruin the film as first-rate parody – but not, fortunately, as propaganda. Brooks never lets his audience forget it is watching a piece of inspired, scatological rubbish aimed straight at Hollywood's exploitative myth-making. And the point is finally made when, in the midst of the

climactic battle scene, Brooks sends a herd of cattle – plus the whole cast – stampeding through the sound-stage wall onto the next set where Dom DeLuise as Buddy Bizarre is presiding over an idiotic Busby Berkeley-style musical epic. After that there is nothing left except for the heroes, Bart and Waco, to ride off into the sunset – in a limousine.

Hollywood, blowing a lot of hot air, turned America's racial problems in the Sixties and Seventies into big box-office. *Blazing Saddles*, noisy, needle-sharp, and irreverent, attempted to puncture the celluloid balloon. Judging from the rude noises that followed, it succeeded.

GEORGE ROBERT KIMBALL

Directed by Mel Brooks, 1974
Prod co: Crossbow, for Warner Brothers. **prod:** Michael Hertzberg. **sc:** Mel Brooks, Norman Steinberg, Andrew Bergman, Richard Pryor, Alan Uger. **titles:** Anthony Goldschmidt. **photo** (Panavision, Technicolor): Joseph Biroc. **sp eff:** Douglas Pettibone. **ed:** John C. Howard, Danford Greene. **prod des:** Peter Wooley. **set dec:** Morey Hoffman. **cost:** Nino Novarese. **mus:** John Morris. **orch:** Jonathan Tunick, John Morris. **songs:** 'Blazing Saddles' by John Morris, Mel Brooks, sung by Frankie Laine, 'I'm Tired', 'The French Mistake', 'The Ballad of Rock Ridge' by Mel Brooks. **chor:** Alan Johnston. **sd:** Gene S. Cantamessa, Arthur Piantadosi, Richard Tyler, Les Fresholtz. **ass dir:** John C. Chulay. **prod man:** William P. Owens. **r/t:** 93 minutes. **Cast:** Cleavon Little (*Black Bart*), Gene Wilder (*the Waco Kid*), Slim Pickens (*Taggart*), Harvey Korman (*Hedley Lamarr*), Madeline Kahn (*Lili Von Shtupp*), Mel Brooks (*Governor William J. Lepetomane/Indian chief*), Burton Gilliam (*Lyle*), Alex Karras (*Mongo*), David Huddleston (*Olson Johnson*), Liam Dunn (*Reverend Johnson*), John Hillerman (*Howard Johnson*), George Furth (*Van Johnson*), Claude Ennis Starrett Jr (*Gabby Johnson*), Carol Arthur (*Harriett Johnson*), Richard Collier (*Dr Sam Johnson*), Charles McGregor (*Charlie*), Robyn Hilton (*Miss Stein*), Don Megowan (*gum chewer*), Dom DeLuise (*Buddy Bizarre*), Count Basie.

'I don't like the term "political" applied to my films, but they are, in a way, the opposite of conventional cinema. They are films of provocation. They attempt to provoke the audience into an awareness of cause and effect.'

So said Francesco Rosi in an interview in the magazine *Time Out*. Yet more than any other contemporary Italian film director, Rosi tackles head-on touchy, political issues. *Salvatore Giuliano* (1961) and *Lucky Luciano* (1973) have looked at the influence of the Mafia; *Mani Sulla Città* (1963, *Hands Over the City*) exposed bad housing and local council corruption in Naples; and *Il Caso Mattei* (1972, *The Mattei Affair*) dealt with international cartels. Rosi's major achievement has been his ability to combine a gripping story-line with hard-hitting, relevant comment, thus stimulating political awareness on a mass, popular level.

Illustrious Corpses is cast in this mould. 'It is a philosophical and political thriller set in an imaginary country which could be England, but is perhaps more like Italy,' said Rosi, making the point that corruption exists everywhere. But the baroque architecture of southern Italy and the modern buildings of Rome locate the film firmly in time and place. The images of corpses in catacombs, busts in museums and other ancient relics that occur throughout suggest a country where antiquity is beautifully preserved but modern life is decaying and polluted.

As the Italian Communist Party (PCI) increased its percentage of votes in elections in the late Sixties, a 'strategy of tension' developed whereby neo-Fascist groups, allegedly linked to top government officials, tried to create a climate of terror and anxiety which they believed would favour the growth of demands for the restoration of law and order under an authoritarian regime. Then, in 1973, Enrico Berlinguer, the General Secretary of the PCI, proposed an 'historic compromise' between Catholics, Socialists and Communists which would unite the centre-ground of Italian politics and isolate the right wing.

This policy of historic compromise further increased the PCI's votes until they were close behind Italy's largest party, the Christian Democrats. But this same policy laid the PCI open to criticism from the Left for abandoning their principles and deserting a revolutionary stance in order to trade for power. It is this political dilemma that *Illustrious Corpses* explores. It takes the 'strategy of tension' for granted and investigates a possible escalation of it.

Rosi makes an unusual choice of hero (a policeman) to represent the common man – someone not directly involved in politics but who gradually finds himself at the centre of a conspiratorial web. Police Inspector Rogas, marvellously played by Lino Ventura, doggedly investigates the deaths of a number of judges in the initial belief that a lone maniac committed the murders. But, as the inquiry continues, he begins to discover the complicity of high-ranking government officials.

When he uncovers evidence of corruption amongst the dead judges, and takes it to his superior, the Chief of Police tears it up, saying that he cannot admit the suggestion of corruption since it would taint the public image of judges as upholders of morality. 'Why not turn your attention to left-wing militants?' he counsels Rogas. As he becomes increasingly powerless in the complex political web, Rogas gradually comes to realize that the aim is to blame the murders on the Left in order to provoke a right-wing *coup d'état*.

At the end of the film the new Communist Party leader refuses to disclose the real cause of his predecessor's death for fear of initiating a riot or upsetting his centrist allies. To justify his inaction, he says 'the truth is not always revolutionary.' It is an ambiguous ending to a film, but one that reflects the real difficulties facing the Left in Italy as it made its historic bid for power.   SALLY HIBBIN

In an unnamed country, public prosecutor Varga (1) is shot dead as he emerges from a visit to the catacombs. Two more judges are killed – one on a highway, one on a city street (2) – even before Varga's funeral (3). Rogas (4), a police inspector, is sent to investigate. He assumes, on advice from his superiors, that a lone maniac is responsible.

Uncovering some corruption relating to a court case, Rogas thinks one of the victims might be guilty. This evidence suggests another judge, Rasto, could be next on the death list. He warns Rasto but does not prevent his death.

Rogas confronts the Chief of Police, who dismisses the inspector's suspicions of corruption, telling him to concentrate on political dissidents. After a visit to the anti-terrorist squad (5), Rogas refuses to work with them and asks to be taken off the case.

Realizing that the Chief Magistrate, Richès, could be in

Directed by Francesco Rosi, 1976
Prod co: Produzioni Europee Associate (Rome)/Les Artistes Associés (Paris). **prod:** Alberto Grimaldi. **prod sup:** Franco Ballati. **sc:** Francesco Rosi, Tonino Guerra, Lino Jannuzzi, based on the novel *Il Conteso* by Leonardo Sciascia. **photo** (Technicolor): Pasquale De Santis. **ed:** Ruggero Mastroianni. **art dir:** Andrea Crisanti. **mus:** Piero Piccioni. **song:** 'Jeanne y Paul' by Astor Piazzolla. **sd:** Enrico Sabbatini. **sd:** Mario Bramonti, Romano Checcacci, Renato Marinelli. **cost:** Mario Bramonti, Romano Checcacci, Renato Marinelli. **ass dir:** Gianni Arduini, Bruno Cortini. **r/t:** 120 minutes. Italian title: *Cadaveri Eccellenti*.
Cast: Lino Ventura (*Inspector Rogas*), Alain Cuny (*Judge Rasto*), Paolo Bonacelli (*Dr Maxia*), Marcel Bozzuffi (*indolent man*), Tina Aumont (*prostitute*), Max Von Sydow (*Chief Magistrate Richès*), Fernando Rey (*Minister of Justice*), Charles Vanel (*Prosecutor Varga*), Renato Salvatori (*police inspector, Rogas' friend*), Tino Carraro (*Chief of Police*), Maria Carta (*Signora Cres*), Luigi Pistilli (*Cusani*), Paolo Graziosi (*Galano, leftist at Patto's party*), Anna Proclemer (*wife of author Nocio*), Carlo Tamberlani (*archbishop*), Enrico Ragusa (*Capuchin monk*), Corrado Gaipa (*supposed mafioso*), Claudio Nicastro (*general*), Francesco Callari (*Judge Sanza*), Mario Meniconi (*mechanic*), Accursio Di Leo (*Rogas' assistant*), Alfonso Gatto (*Nocio*), Silverio Blasi (*chief of political police*), Renato Turi (*television announcer*), Giorgio Zampa (*Amar*), Florestano Vancini (*Amar's successor*), Ernesto Colli (*agent*), Alexandre Mnouchkine (*Pattos*), Felice Fulchignoni (*mayor*).

'SENSATIONAL' SUNDAY TIMES

Illustrious CORPSES
A Film by FRANCESCO ROSI (The Mattei Affair)
Subtitles   Released by Cinegate Ltd.

4

7

danger, Rogas tries to warn him, but is surprised to find cars belonging to the heads of the armed forces and the Chief of Police outside Richès' apartment. Rogas later meets Richès (6), who lectures him on the absolute authority of the law.

At a party (7) the Minister of Justice and a powerful ship-owner both suggest to Rogas that if a left-wing suspect were nailed it would prove politically useful. Richès is also shot (8). With the help of Cusani, a journalist friend, Rogas arranges a meeting at the Roman Museum (9) with Amar, leader of the Italian Communist Party, so as to reveal his suspicions that the Right are trying to provoke a *coup d'état*. Rogas and Amar are both killed and the murder is blamed on Rogas' unbalanced state of mind. Amar's successor refuses to reveal the truth.

1

2

3

5

6

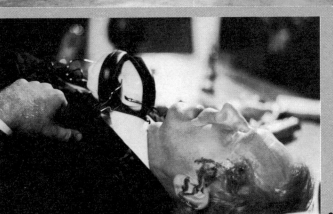

8

9